H. G. Adler

THE JEWS IN GERMANY

From the Enlightenment to National Socialism

UNIVERSITY OF NOTRE DAME PRESS
NOTRE DAME LONDON

Originally published by
Kösel Verlag, © 1960 as
Die Juden in Deutschland: Von der Aufklärung bis zum Nationalsozialismus

Library of Congress Catalog Card Number: 69–14814
Manufactured in the United States of America

PREFACE

There is a long history to the murderous attitude of National Socialism toward the Jew. Its source lies much further back than the beginning in 1870–80 of the antisemitic movement, which gave the hatred of Jews its essentially "biological," "racist," and "scientific" underpinnings and thus gave it the character of a *Weltanschauung*, an ideology and finally a demoniacal-eschatological theory of salvation. The modern form of the hatred of the Jew developed in Germany throughout the entire Age of Emancipation (1780–1933). It grew in other countries as well, but chiefly in Germany. It was the result, for the most part, of conditions that surrounded the granting of civic equality to the Jews in the German countries, the result of the emancipators' intentions of destroying or eroding all Jewish characteristics and Jewish ethnic feeling. It was, in other words, the result of an equality never granted completely or sincerely. More than anything else, it sprang from an impatience that was felt on all sides. The aim of this book is to elucidate this process. At the same time, I hope the book will shed the light of greater understanding on the reasons for the German origin of the holocaust which overtook all of Europe's Jewry after 1933.

In order to avoid misunderstanding and misinterpretation, it must be said that this book is a guide to historical problems, not a history—even in outline form—of the Jews in Germany. It is not and could not have been an exhaustive presentation; rather it represents a conscious selection of themes that at present agitate many Germans when they contemplate the special character and fate of their Jewish minority. Circumstances not treated here are not thereby to be thought of as unimportant. But they have to be left for future treatment, since they could not be managed in this deliberately concise guide for today's readers. My book, therefore, cannot do full justice to the whole problem.

London
May, 1961

CONTENTS

I

A SURVEY OF THE PROBLEM: AN INTRODUCTION

Jews have been living among Germans since the origin of the German state at the time of Charlemagne. Often but not always a difficult coexistence, it has always created special problems, whose various remedies have proven neither satisfactory over the long run nor permanent. The Jewish-German relationship during its first five hundred years had much in common with the Jewish situation in most other Western Christian countries. Although eventually to change, much of this common European form survived in Germany until the late nineteenth and into the twentieth century. The first three hundred years of coexistence—from roughly the foundation of the empire to the First Crusade in 1096 or perhaps somewhat later—was much less severe, with some exceptions, than it became. The position of the Jews worsened when the power of the emperor to hold his empire together diminished, and the realm more and more took on the appearance of a loose confederation rather than a centrally-controlled state. This sad development, which in many ways still influences German history, was not the sole or chief reason for the difficulties of the Jewish minority. The communities of the Jews were attacked as the hordes of the First Crusade swept through Germany, burning, killing, and robbing. These crusaders came from France, and Frenchmen thus first broke the peace, but German noblemen and commoners participated in the outrages.

It was at this time that the form of the question that would remain valid into the Age of Emancipation was shaped: The possibility of a Jewish minority existing in a Christian state, given that the Jews followed a despised foreign religion and were clearly distinguished from the ruling nation in language, culture, tradition, and socioeconomic structure. A good many countries, after periods of severe hardship for the Jews, banished them altogether: England, 1290; France, 1306, and, after a period of readmission, again in 1394; Spain, 1492; Portugal, 1497. Like Italy, Germany never undertook a wholesale exile, although numerous secular and clerical German sovereigns expelled the Jews, just as was done in cities subject only to the emperor. This was the situation (Frankfurt was an exception) approximately until the end of the fifteenth century. These restrictions were finally overcome, as were those in German countries where the right of settlement was specifically limited to certain areas, during the nineteenth century, four cities in Baden state being the last to lift them in 1862. Despite this general picture, neither emperor nor princes ever wanted to be rid entirely of the tribute-paying Jews. The pecuniary motive explains the continuity of Jewish history in Germany, where it was uninterrupted, as was not the case in other countries: excepting the Crypto-Jews (Marranos), there were no Jews in the Iberian countries from the end of the fifteenth century until legal readmission to Spain in 1868 and to Portugal a little later. In England there is certainly no Jewish history until 1655 or official Jewish readmission in 1663.

The history of minorities unprotected by treaty and subject to unlimited despotism, who neither can nor want to conform to the majority, has always been a history of repression, tolerable perhaps or perhaps insupportable. In Germany the conditions of the Jews during the High Middle Ages moved gradually toward the intolerable, reaching full measure of stringency in the period from the thirteenth to the sixteenth century. In the seventeenth century, undoubtedly as a result of the devastation of the Thirty Years' War, there were ameliorations with occasional setbacks. Finally, Jews achieved liberation in the sense of the emancipation of their middle class, the fruit of a period in which brute force and brutal threats played lesser roles than previously. Liberation was sealed by the Constitution of the North German Federation on July 3, 1869, and confirmed for all of Germany, including Bavaria, by the Constitution of the Second Empire. Until then, Bavaria had been backward in this respect. Germany, however, was preceded by nearly all the countries of the civilized West: first, the United States, equality coming with independence; France, 1791; then Holland, Belgium, Denmark, Sweden, Italy, and finally, the Austro-Hungarian monarchy in 1867.

The principle adopted by Germany for the emancipation was the dangerous one formulated by Clermont-Tonnerre in the French Convention: "We must refuse everything to the Jews as a Nation, but must grant the Jews everything as individuals." Adopted and first implemented by Napoleon, this principle is still the standard that governs the position of the Jewish minority in the civic structure of Germany. There was no question of the recognition of the minority as an ethnic group or of placing Jews on equal footing with other citizens. Recognition was for single individuals and came at a time when religious ties were weakening in general and when the state at least was becoming more secular. Thus, on the other side, the deep-going changes in the social and cultural situation of the Jews in Western countries reaching to the Russian and Austro-Polish borders went far toward meeting the aims of the emancipators. While social and spiritual isolation had been forced upon the Jews, it is undeniable that it had been to some extent a group desire. This changed entirely in the age of the enlightenment and mercantilism. Led by a few intellectuals, Jewish youth were unsatisfied with their backward conditions. While the modern secular state could not tolerate within itself a non-conforming individual splinter group, the minority itself no longer wished to live according to its outmoded social forms which, moreover, were undignified. On this basis, the Jew was ready to give up much, often everything. Civic equality was purchased by this sacrifice, which was made by the leading strata of the minority at least.

At various times since the end of the eighteenth century, it has seemed that the Jewish minority would eliminate itself by means of assimilation. Felix Teilhaber, a Jewish scholar, predicted the self-destruction of the Jews by the end of the twentieth century (*Der Untergang der deutschen Juden*, "The Disappearance of the German Jews," 1911). Population statistics seemed to bear out his projection. There were approximately 270,000 Jews in Germany in 1829, or 1.9 per cent. In 1871 there were 512,000, or 1.25 per cent; in 1900, 587,000, or 1.14 per cent; in 1910, 615,000, or 0.95 per cent; in 1925, 564,000, or 0.9 per cent. There were only 499,000 Jews in Germany in 1933. Moreover, between 1880 and 1900, there was an immigration to Germany of 47,000 Jews from the Slavic countries; in 1925, about 108,000 Jews of other nationalities were living in the country. By conversion, mixed marriage, childlessness, and emigration, then, the relative percentage and, later, the actual percentage of Jews in the general population declined during the Age of Emancipation. Without the influx of immigrants, the loss would have been considerably more noticeable.

By the late eighteenth century, the minority desired nothing so much as to be German, especially after the voluntary emancipation undertaken by a large German state through the Edict of Hardenburg (1812) (withdrawn, however, four years later). The minority asked for only a certain amount of independent religious activity, although there was an inclination from the start toward making sometimes dreadful concessions on this point. Germanization ("*Deutschtum*") was cultivated throughout the nineteenth century and into the twentieth century, and it remained the Jewish aim even after emancipation was itself repealed by the laws and ordinances of 1933 and by the Reich citizenship law of 1935.

How then did a truly Jewish question survive in the face of this voluntary assimilation and the profound national and ethnic self-destruction of the minority? There have been many answers to this question, some illuminating, some obscuring the problem. I shall venture to formulate a definite reply: Impatience was the main cause of the premature failure of Jewish emancipation in Germany. More than assimilation was asked of the Jews; they were asked to conform completely, which would have meant the abdication of every kind of individualism and which would have been a kind of extinction. The Jews could not possibly assimilate quickly enough for their enemies, hasten as they might. Deficiencies in the social behavior of the Jews of Germany—sometimes real deficiencies, sometimes not—were seized upon first to deny civil equality, then to postpone and temporize over concessions. When emancipation became law, it was rarely, if ever, completely implemented and yet was attacked by the most unrestrained calumnies against the Jews. In the so-called Antisemitism Petition, submitted to Bismarck in 1881, the repeal of emancipation was demanded twelve years after its enactment:

> For some time the minds and spirits of serious, patriotic men of all ways of life and all parties have been troubled by the unchecked growth of the Jewish ethnic element. The much-hoped-for amalgamation of Semitic and Germanic elements has, despite equality, proved a chimera.

This is not the place to weigh the truth or judge the sincerity of this statement. It is clear, however, that an impossible demand was being made. The necessary and desired blending was simply assumed to be a failure, like so many vain hopes; yet amalgamation had hardly been tried. This was not the way to solve the difficulties of assimilation however great they might be. It made them only more acute. Despite the attempts, then, at improvement during the period under consideration (1780–1930), a catastrophe was in the making. Only by understanding this can the backfiring of emancipation in Germany be understood; we propose, therefore, to explain it in more detail. Instead of assimilation and equality, the fate of the Jews was to be alienation and hatred. Five years of National Socialism served to nullify Jewish emancipation and do away with the possibility of a Jew's earning even a livelihood; five additional years saw, not only expulsion, but Jewish destruction. In the years before National Socialism the Jews had not been given time enough to meet the demands, just or unjust, set as conditions for their

for such undertakings; the scholar will look in vain for similar evidence from the thirteenth to eighteenth century.

From the First Crusade until after the Reformation, the situation of the Jews in Germany constantly grew worse. It then stabilized for a century, began to improve somewhat after 1648 and through the Age of Pietism and Enlightenment. Improvement, however, was felt only by a privileged few, the rest of the Jewish group continuing without any kind of settled rights. The loss of rights had been a gradual process. How had it come about?

Until the First Crusade and after, the German clergy, many kings, princes, and free cities (with their citizens) were tolerant. When the horror stories from France reached Germany during the collections for the First Crusade, Henry IV issued an edict to his secular and clerical princes for the purpose of protecting the Jews. It had little effect. In Metz, Trier, Worms, Mainz, Regensburg, Prague, and other communities, thousands of Jews were murdered. The crusaders appeared to act on the feeling: "We are setting out on the long and arduous path to conquer the Holy Tomb. Shall we permit those who killed our Savior to live among us?" Thence until early in the sixteenth century, the bloodbaths staged against the Jews were numerous in Germany, the victims many. Superficially, the carnage can be explained as religious fanaticism proceeding from theological considerations—retribution for the alleged defiling of the host, the alleged murders of Christians, of young boys whose blood was supposed to be employed for purposes of ritual, and the alleged spreading of pestilences by the poisoning of wells. In fact, however, there were often primitive economic reasons behind the thievery and slaughter. Following the First

Crusade, the general peace established in 1103 reaffirmed the previous conditions of the Jews, and this was shortly after backed by papal bull.

Although St. Bernard of Clairvaux called the lending of money "*iudaizare*," an expression that had disastrous consequences, his intervention preserved the relative safety of the Jews during the Second Crusade. Then, in 1215, moneylending was forbidden as a Christian profession and the role was forced upon the Jews, who were becoming more and more subject to proscriptions. They were ordered to wear special clothing, including the "Jewish hat," and other distinguishing signs. Strict geographic separation was set in motion, although it was only later, in 1350, that Jews were forced to live in walled sections in houses that were city property or under lease by the city. The Frankfurt Ghetto was closed off only in 1462. Personal social intercourse between Jews and Christians virtually ended with the prohibitions on common meals, games, feasts, baths, and inns. Even religious dialogue was forbidden. The apparent reason for this proscription were the several attested voluntary conversions of Germans, including clergymen, to Judaism between 817 and the later times of worse persecution. The most devastating consequences for the Jews, however, stemmed from their nearly total exclusion from all honorable professions in the crafts, agriculture, and in most types of commerce. The Jews came rapidly under the onus of usury. The actual situation is revealed in this document of privilegization granted by Frederick III in 1470:

> Where the Christian takes ten shock a year, the Jew is permitted to take twenty, because he could not make a living if he took as little as the Christian (1) because he has to fulfill his obligations toward us; (2) because he has

to pay the lord who has been made his protector; (3) because he has to audit the interests; (4) because seldom does an authority whose service he needs let him go without payment; and, finally, because he himself has to have something to be able to live on with his wife and children. [Palacký, Vol. V, Part 1, p. 445.]

The emperors always considered the Jews as their personal property. While Jews could not be given away, mortgaged, inherited, or sold, they were under obligation to pay their owner—secular or clerical—heavily in order merely to live. The Emperor Frederick II called the Jews "serfs of the imperial chambers." From this there devolved the obligations to pay an annual tax, extraordinary expenses, and penalties, which under the Hohenstaufen and later grew to the proportions of an unbearable burden upon the Jews. Soon the only accepted or remembered status of the Jews was that princes and cities had rights over them which had been passed on to the Electoral Princes by the Golden Bull. The imperial head tax, independent of other contributions to the reigning prince, was introduced by Ludwig the Bavarian. It continued to be collected until 1806 in cities under imperial sovereignty. If a Jew left his place of residence without authorization, all his property was forfeit. Again, it was Ludwig who declared that "the Jews belong to us and the empire in body, soul, and earthly goods, . . . we can do with them as we please and as we find convenient." (Elbogen, p. 55.)

The year 1349 was the worst year for the Jews in Germany until Hitler. There is solid evidence of the entire Jewish population being slaughtered, mostly by burning, in more than 350 communities. Using the precedent established by Ludwig, Charles IV had negotiated treaties that gave carte blanche to the murder of Jews so long as the emperor was recompensed for the loss. Such a treaty was signed June 25, 1349, with Frankfurt, a month before the mass murder there. The city pledged 12,000 hellers and part of the property of the slain to the emperor. The empty treasuries of emperors and cities explain this behavior much more adequately than do notions of the fear of pestilences spread by "the poisoning of wells by Jews." This fantasy had not even reached Nuremberg when, following a treaty concluded with Charles, some 570 Jews were slaughtered. In Mainz the Jews were slaughtered, but only after several days of heroic resistance. In Cologne they very often killed themselves by throwing themselves into the flames. Baptism was frequently an alternative to death; for the most part this escape was rarely chosen, and the Jews remained steadfast in their faith.

Thereafter, expulsions became the rule. When a Jew was granted "unlimited" readmission to a place, despite a general expulsion, it would continue valid only a short time: ten to twelve years was considered favorable, but each prolongation had to be bought dearly. Moreover, there was a tax on departure. In 1390–91 King Wenceslaus waived all debts to the Jews over to the cities, who paid him considerable sums, but the procedure was of little aid to debtors, who found the cities to be more powerful collectors than the Jews. There was a substantial Jewish emigration from Germany to Poland, Italy, and Turkey during the fourteenth to the sixteenth century, but some Jews held on, particularly in the western and southern parts of the empire. A time of abject servitude followed the period of mass murders, and with it came an attitude of incredible acceptance. The heroism that had been maintained in the face of the persecutions began to give way to the wretchedness of a pariah existence.

The enunciation of new principles, such as those proposed

by Reuchlin in his famous assessment of Jewish literature in 1510, had little effect on the real situation. He had written: "We as well as they are citizens of the same Roman empire and enjoy the same civic rights and the same peace." And: "They are not members of the church and therefore their faith is none of our business." The young Luther, too, was sympathetic to the Jews at first, albeit he was motivated by a zeal for conversion, unlike Reuchlin, and turned on the Jews savagely when they refused his attempts to bring them into the reformed church.

> They are living in our home, [he wrote] under our protection and patronage, . . . and princes and superiors hold still . . . letting the Jews steal them blind as they please; that is, they permit themselves and their subjects to be sucked dry and be made beggars with their own money. And yet, to this day, we do not know what kind of devil brought them to our country. . . . They may leave for their own country whenever they want, and we shall be glad to give them presents in order to be rid of them.

This is language frighteningly similar to Hitler's nearly four hundred years later. And Luther's anger over his rebuff has been instrumental in shaping the plight of Jews in Protestant countries, where they have often fared worse than in Catholic regions.

Court Jews emerged in the sixteenth century. These were men of financial acumen who were personally empowered by a prince to administer his money and property. Some of them were highly regarded; others, like the unfortunate Suess, came to fearful ends. At first, their prominence affected the rest of their group very little, but some started family traditions that would later help smoothe the way toward changing public opinion during the Enlightenment. This very thin upper layer was the one best fitted—by reasons of language, education, and attitudes—for the kind of assimilation that was made the prerequisite of emancipation. Another favorable development was the granting of complete sovereignty to all imperial estates after the Thirty Years' War (which itself had not appreciably worsened the Jewish situation). There was now an interest, not only in Court Jews, chief stewards, financial agents, and clerks, but in Jews who could contribute to commerce and manufacture. Thus, there arose a scattering of rich Jews, a small middle class occupied in whatever commerce lay outside the scope of guild regulations. But there was also the preponderant mass, living in misery, pursuing meaningless occupations that offered little real hope of financial improvement.

The policy of the Grand Elector may serve here as a typical case. Ninety-eight years after the "perpetual" expulsion of Jews from Brandenburg, the Grand Elector in 1671 again accepted Jews. But they must be rich. In return they were allowed relatively favorable conditions: permission to rent free-dwellings, to build or buy houses; to participate in open shops and at fairs in wool, textile goods, and meat trading; taxes and tributes were to be no higher than those of Christians; the head tax was waived; instead there was a family protective tax of eight thalers per year; a gold guilder was to be paid for each marriage; and private, but not public, religious services were permissible. Although these practical measures derived from prosaic motives, theology too had some influence on the Jewish fate before emancipation. As late as 1700, the Pietist Spener held that Jews should be given the opportunity to convert by being permitted to live among Christians.

III

THE SITUATION OF THE JEWS CIRCA 1780

Every Jew living in the empire in the period around 1780 was the subject of restrictive exceptional laws that weighed most heavily on the mass of the group. But even the few Jews whose lives were easier by virtue of wealth or fame were greatly limited in their personal freedom. In general, the Jew was an object of scorn. In the common view they were a race of beggars, peddlers, usurers; they were unlikable, deeply superstitious, uneducated, and grotesque in appearance and behavior. This was Goethe's impression of the Jews who lived in the narrow streets of his native Frankfurt; it was a view he could not shake, despite his later friendly acquaintances with Jews and descendants of Jews whose appearance was completely different from the memories that had hardened into stereotype.

The year 1780 was the twenty-sixth year of the friendship of the poet Lessing and the dwarfed, hunchbacked Moses Mendelssohn of Dessau, whom Lessing immortalized in the figure of Nathan the Wise. Mendelssohn was an astonishing man, although he can hardly be called an originator of the great caliber of numerous Jewish philosophers, scholars, and writers who came later. He had, however, a human greatness that stands comparison with other elect minds. In the face of personal poverty and an unprotected civic status (he was tolerated in Berlin but had no letter of privilege and was therefore under constant threat of expulsion), despite his early lack of knowledge of German, he persevered to become a fine writer in German and earned the undivided respect and veneration of educated people all over Germany. He was an example for the Jews of Germany, but his influence extended beyond the borders of the empire. Christian sympathizers saw in him the living proof of the falsity of the prejudice against the Jews and of the need to improve and bring up to standard the lot of his people, both socially and in civic rights. Emancipation would have come without Mendelssohn, but he helped its coming considerably. It is not a mere coincidence that Prussia, under no French influence, led the progressive movement and proclaimed Jewish equality in civic rights before any other German country, twenty-six years after the death of Mendelssohn.

During the period of Mendelssohn's life, however, every Jew paid a head- or convoy tax at the border of each of the three hundred states of the empire. Mendelssohn himself paid the charge in 1776. It amounted to the tax on the importation of one bull from Poland. The cities levied similar taxes, waiving them only for privileged Jews traveling within their home states. In Saxony, the so-called Jewish Ordinance was in force, according to which only a certain number of Jews were permitted to dwell in Dresden and Leipzig, paying for the privilege a protection fee of seventy thalers per head of family, thirty thalers for the wife, and five thalers for each child. Each license to marry cost forty thalers. Jews were allowed to ply only the occupations of moneylending and the second-hand sale of clothing. In Bavaria, Jews could enter most places only for short stays, their business being transacted under supervision of the police, called in Nuremberg the "living convoy." In Frankfurt, with five hundred Jewish families, twelve marriages were permitted in any one year. The obligation to doff the hat whenever a Christian called out to a Jew in the street: "Your manners, Jew!" still remained effective around 1780. Although the requirement of wearing a distinguishing sign upon the outward clothing had been generally abandoned by 1728, it was officially abolished in Frankfurt only in that year. The situation was better in Hamburg, where the Marranos, who had immigrated before 1600, developed into a booming community as Catholic "Merchants of Portuguese Nationality."

In Fürth, where Jews had been accepted after their expulsion from Nuremberg, conditions were relatively good. They had the right to elect two deputies to the city assembly, to trade in a variety of merchandise, and to follow crafts, but only to satisfy their own community's needs. They might maintain their own musicians. Their commercial freedom was further extended during the eighteenth century and, moreover, there was a Jewish hospital, Jewish physicians, and—unique at the time—a pharmacy. Fürth was the example held up by the first great advocate of emancipation, the Prussian councilor Christian Wilhelm von Dohm (about whom there is more to follow) to demonstrate the feasibility and desirability of improving the civic status of the Jews.

In Berlin the Jewish population had grown since the time of the Great Elector but conditions were bad, despite the work of the Commission on the Jews, which had pioneered a more tolerant attitude. Frederick William I and Frederick II were no friends of the Jews. In 1750, Frederick promulgated his Revised General Privilege and Rule (to place this in context, it comes after Lessing's advocacy of the Jewish cause in his comedy, *The Jews*, but antedates his friendship with Moses Mendelssohn). In a broad way the general lines of the "rule" held for the next fifty years. It read:

> For the settlement of Jews . . . the following principles should be kept in mind: (1) A distinction is to be made between the Jews under protection and those who are tolerated outside the order of the country. (2) The . . . extraordinary privileged Jews are not permitted to settle a child or to be married at their place of residence on the basis of right. (3) If a Jew who is privileged passes away, the privilege reverts to his oldest child; its . . . siblings, however, cannot enjoy further protection in consequence of this. (4) The regular privileged Jew is permitted to include as privileged one child during his lifetime (but is not allowed to change the choice once it has been made) and enter its name in the letter of privilege and give it in marriage, if documents are presented ahead of time. (5) Foreign Jews should not be permitted to settle in our country; such may ask our permission, however, if he has a fortune of 10,000 thalers and is willing to bring it with him. (6) Public servants, seal engravers, eyeglass makers, optical-glass grinders, painters, and others who earn their living through one of the occupations open to Jews, or those maintained by the Jewish community alone, may not only exercise no other commerce than the craft which they have mastered, but they cannot be considered as extraordinarily privileged Jews and cannot be entered as such. . . . We—seriously—order: That no Jew exercise a guild craft nor assume anything else but seal engraving, painting, grinding of optical glass, diamonds, or stones, embroidery

of gold and silver, sewing of white goods, cleaning of metal shavings, and similar crafts in which there are no guilds or professional associations; above all, Jews must not brew beer or distil alcohol.

Without our express permission, our Berlin-protected Jews must have nothing to do with commerce in, or manufacture of, raw wool, woolen yarn, and manufactured goods from wool. In addition, all foreign Jews who come on foot or horseback, and who do not arrive by the post coach or special coaches, must enter by no gate other than the Prenzlau or Halle, and their ingress to other cities should be regulated as much as possible by access through specially designated gates. In general, no foreign Jew is to be admitted unless he is in possession of a passport or of proof of his originating point and the reasons for his travels. If a Jew lends money on note, he is entitled to twelve per cent, if the note is for twelve months or less; but whenever a capital of one hundred thalers or more is in question and is borrowed for a year against interest, he is not entitled to more than eight per cent, under threat of losing the capital. Protected Jews who do not own their own houses should not be licensed to purchase any. . . . As there are forty houses in Berlin registered to Jewish owners, this is the number that should remain in force . . . and this number should never be increased. Jews cannot buy land or own landed property. [Hoxter, pp. 184 ff.]

To supervise the enforcement of these rules, there was a general board made up of members of the ministries of interior and finance. The regularly protected Jews were given letters of license, naming place of residence, occupation, and the other members of their family who were under protection. Irregular or "extraordinary" protected Jews were safe for the span of their lifetime in their own person, at a certain place of residence, and in a specified occupation. The status of tolerated Jew went to community functionaries, rabbis, temple-readers, and ritual butchers; such also were their children and the children of the Jews under extraordinary protection. The annual income from the payments for protection amounted to some 25,000 thalers. In addition, there was a recruiting tax, a silver tax (whose operation is unknown), a tax on voting that was collected every third year, a fire-protection tax, a tax on rubber stamps, and many other taxes. The marriage tax varied between twenty and eighty thalers; marriage certificates cost an additional fourteen thalers. The registration of children cost up to 160 thalers. There was a tax for escort upon any move from one Prussian county to another. In 1769, the notorious "export of china" tax was introduced. It was exacted on every marriage contract, house purchase, or other contract made under civil law. It consisted of the required purchase from an imperial manufactory of up to three hundred thalers of porcelain to be sold abroad. It could be sold thus only at highly unfavorable terms. Jews lost some 100,000 thalers in this way during the course of eight years. For the general right to settle a second child, Frederick II required the payment of 70,000 thalers. Additionally, 1,500 thalers worth of textiles had to be purchased for export in each case. This bizarre export tax was abolished in 1788, in exchange for Jewish assumption of the control of the textile mills, which had been losing ventures.

Pressure upon and persecution of the Jews was unceasing. It influenced everyday matters and behavior in the smallest and most ridiculous details. Except for the rich, who could purchase favors, the situation was intolerable. While the situation was not everywhere like the Prussian situation, the result was the same: an extremity of restriction and pressure. Whatever rubric the taxes and assessments were paraded under, they were simply enforced sacrifices and penalties. The authorities, for example, in Chur-Mainz levied the following taxes in addition to assessments for lighting the Jewish street: for the salaries of the Jewish community magistrates; for the poorhouse and the cemetery; for New Year presents; for a goose at the Feast of St. Martin; for the arch-priest; for ringing the bells in the parish of St. Emeran; for poor students in the Jesuit study house; for fish money for the Franciscans, the Capuchins, and Jesuits; for the field guards; and for the "pike which is presented to the rector of the university during Holy Week."

The structure of the Jewish ethnic minority reflected the imposition of these painful regulations. While the Jews lived within communities that retained a modicum of internal autonomy, the frame of their personal lives was extremely restricted. A closed system of rabbinical regulations governed not only religion but every aspect of social existence, including education. Elbogen, the Jewish historian, has remarked: "To suffer and learn to harden one's self, on the one hand; to pray, study the holy works, and meditate, on the other: these were the two poles within which Jewish life took its course." (Elbogen, p. 174.) If we are to understand who or what was responsible for this pitiable general condition, the extraordinary obstacles in the way of establishing a more dignified kind of existence have to be taken into account. Yet it was just this kind of existence that troubled and embarrassed the enlightened people—and the authorities as well—who were now beginning to take an interest in the Jews. They did not think that Moses Mendelssohn constituted a problem. The problem they saw was in the medieval attitude which prevailed among the Jews and to which the Jews clung up to the eve of the beginning of the movement for emancipation. They had been condemned to these conditions by the princes.

Yet the speed with which this anachronistic existence disintegrated was astonishing. It was perfectly intact everywhere except in Berlin around 1780. Twenty years later, most of the Jews, particularly the young, had left it behind. The non-Jews who sympathized with the Jewish plight had hoped for Jewish "enlightenment." After 1780 it occurred with almost precipitous rapidity. The upgrading of Jewish education had been a demand for years, especially in Berlin. Mendelssohn himself had pioneered in this field by his German and Hebrew writings and by his translations into German. While conservative rabbis saw danger or even sin in Mendelssohn's translating Old Testament texts into German, their protests went unheeded in the new winds of change. Then, in 1778, two followers of Mendelssohn founded the Jewish Free School. The language of instruction was to be German, not Yiddish. A thin, upper layer of educated Germans and Jews were now finding a path toward each other. Together, they would take up the cause of the emancipation of the Jewish community, or nation (as it was now called), and give it powerful impetus.

IV

THE FIRST REFORMS

The tremendous sudden push to adapt the medieval and outmoded life of the Jews, rich and poor, to modern conditions was an amalgam—of the teachings of a natural law common to all men; of the Enlightenment, with its optimism about progress and the educability of the race, including its most backward groups; of the changes involved in the transition from mercantilism to capitalism and from the corporate to the constitutional state. Adaptation was the watchword of every Jew and non-Jew who strove for Jewish emancipation. Among Jews as a whole, there was a strong opposition to this trend only at first; among non-Jews in German lands there was a mammoth resistance up to emancipation itself.

Non-Jews who wished for Jewish emancipation strove generally for a gradual kind of adaptation, but they continuously found fault with Jewish separatism, with Jewish differences of whatever form, even religious, which fitted as it had been for a life of steady persecution and oppression (or isolation at best) was hardly suited to an enlightened secular state. But Jewish emancipationists, on the other hand, were ready for the most far-reaching and rapid kind of accommodation: they were prepared to jettison everything—except their religion. Their religion, even if it were to become voluntary and be profoundly reformed, could not be abandoned altogether if Jews were to remain Jews. Jews could not accept emancipation for themselves on any other terms. Or emancipation would merely have been the civil equalization of persons of Jewish descent who were no longer Jews. This was, indeed, the aim of the German emancipators. The coincidence of the drive for emancipation with the development of the national state contained this inherent threat to Western Jews in general and—as we now know—this downright calamitous threat to German Jews: the national states' inherently inimical attitude to any minorities within it. Jews particularly suffered from this impulse, because they were without a permanent geographic homeland and because in the economic sense they had been forced into a special kind of existence. The most well-meaning reformers could not free them without enormous difficulties.

We have anticipated our story somewhat in order to emphasize that the first attempts at emancipation manifested simply the kind of idealism that spurs people of good will anywhere anytime to rectify abuse. It was an idealism without concrete social or political program. When the Jews of Alsace prepared a petition for presentation to the king of France by Moses Mendelssohn, he conferred with the Prussian councilor, Christian Wilhelm Dohm. Their thoughts of the time are expressed in Dohm's *On the Civic Improvement of the Jews* (1781). Without denying Jewish deficiencies, he related them to the rightless condition of the Jews. On this basis Dohm called for new laws aiming at the early, complete emancipation of the Jews. In an impressive canvas, he portrayed Jewish life in the German states:

In some [states] . . . they were denied residence and only the traveler was permitted, against payment of a certain sum, to enjoy the protection of the sovereign. In most [states] . . . Jews were accepted under most cumbersome regulations. Only a certain number of Jewish families . . . are allowed to settle, and this permission is restricted to certain places and each time . . . has to be bought with a considerable sum of money. If a Jewish father has several sons . . . he can pass on the favorable circumstances of his existence in the country of his birth . . . only to one of them . . . , the others must be sent to strange regions where they encounter the same unfavorable restrictions. As for his daughters, everything depends on his being lucky enough to introduce them into the few families at his place of residence. . . . Once a Jew has received permission to remain in a state, he has to buy it again every year by means of a heavy tax; he cannot marry without special permission . . . and without new expenses; each child increases the amount of his taxes and nearly all of his actions are taxable. . . . In view of these varied taxes, the earning power of the Jew is extremely limited. . . . Agriculture is everywhere forbidden to him, and nearly nowhere can he own real property. Every guild would consider itself dishonored if it should accept a circumcised one as one of theirs. . . . It is only rare genius which retains the energy and courage, in the face of such adverse conditions, to raise itself to the arts and letters. . . . And even those rare persons who achieve a high degree of competence in the arts or letters, as well as those who would honor mankind by their blameless probity, are only able to win the respect of a few aristocrats. In the eyes of the masses, not even the most outstanding merits of heart and mind can obliterate the one defect, the unpardonable sin of being a Jew. . . . These unfortunates have no other avenue left to them but com-

> merce. But this, too, is made difficult by many taxes and restrictions. . . . They therefore are restricted to small retailing . . . or they are forced to lend their money. [Dohm, *op. cit.*]

To this dark catalogue, Dohm brings forward the advantages that would lie in a fair treatment of the Jews:

> Our states should welcome any citizen who observes the law and who, by his own diligence, increases the riches of the state. The Jew, too, is entitled to this enjoyment, to this love. His religion does not render him unworthy of this. . . . Who can help but have high respect for the Jew whom no torture or martyrdom can induce to give up his religious laws or, on the other hand, detest the worthless one who for monetary advantage denies his religion and pays lip service to the Christian one? The clinging to the age-old faith alone imparts to the Jews a stability which is a great advantage in the formation of their morality. . . . They are always devoted to the state and often have shown a zeal in danger which could hardly have been expected from members of society so little favored as they. [*Ibid.*]

At this point in time Dohm is ready to concede the Jews their own religion; later this was rarely to be true among reformers. Emancipation was seldom again to be viewed from this sort of humanitarian standpoint. The question then arose (this was still during Mendelssohn's time) of whether the Jews were a people. Up to 1800 it had been conventional to call them a "nation," "colony," or "the Jewish class." Not long after, the appellations "citizens of Jewish faith," "Mosaites," and "Israelites" became popular except with the enemies of emancipation. A well-intentioned emancipationist declared in 1808: "Since religious fanaticism has lost much of its power today and as equal rights are established by law, the convention of the Jew as a nation should disappear completely." (Schmidt as quoted in *Europäische Staats-Relationen,* 1808, Vol. XI, "In wie weit können die Juden noch eine Nation genannt werden.") Another, anonymous, writer optimistically put it this way in 1799: "It may . . . be assumed that the enlightened Jew is already essentially a Christian and that he only lacks the characteristics of a Christian which are especially to be desired . . . because they do not restrict man so much in his natural rights and liberties." (Schmidt, p. 31; from *Denkwürdigkeiten und Tagesgeschichten der Mark Brandenburg,* June, 1799.)

A certain Bran demanded energetic self-reform in 1807: "Masters of Israel! Do not think that simplifying the ceremonies, abolishing feast days, and destroying superstitions is enough. Mankind demands more from you, and the spirit of the times will have its revenge if you disappoint the expectations of rational people." (Schmidt, p. 37; from *Europäische Staats-Relationen,* 1808, Vol. XI, "Über bürgerliche Erziehung.") Education was frequently seen as the road to assimilation, as this material from Vogt stresses:

> Education . . . is the only way to assimilate the rest of this unhappy nation with the Europeans. The Jews must be cleared of certain characteristics and customs in the interest of emancipation. First, they must be denied the name of a nation insofar as civic rights are concerned. Second, such institutions of theirs which refer to them as an independent, sovereign people must be abolished. Their only valid laws are to be their purely religious laws. Third, they must obey all the laws, duties, and customs to which every citizen is subject. Fourth, the Jews must try to assimilate the education of their children to that of children in the public schools. [Schmidt, p. 38; from *Europäische Staats-Relationen,* 1808, Vol. XI.]

Actually, very few reforms occurred for twenty-five years from the publication of Dohm's already-quoted work. A draft bill submitted to the French king in 1790 that requested Jews to be equal to Christians "with the exception of a very few religious differences, within sixty-seventy years" (Dubnow, p. 184) was so innocuous that David Friedländer, Mendelssohn's disciple and spokesman of the Jews, rejected it. In 1793, a royal commission opined:

> Experience has shown that the Jew can exercise every civic virtue. If his heart be not hardened by misery and persecution, he is able to show his fellow citizens, regardless of religion, as much good will, willingness to sacrifice, unselfishness, and self-denial, as anyone else. There is some foundation to the belief that Jews are rather inclined to excessive goodness. [Valentin, p. 33.]

But nothing really changed, except that the head tax and collective liability for taxes were abolished in 1793, followed by abolition in 1801 of the collective liability for theft.

However, in the upper strata of society, particularly in Berlin, the assimilationist process of national dissolution was making slow progress. Lazarus Ben-David, another disciple of Mendelssohn, in 1793 described the Jews as divided into four groups: the "true believers," fossilized and unable to assimilate. They were dying out. Second, the "libertines," baptized but shunned by Christians; third and fourth, the "educated" and "partly educated," who could be counted on to re-establish a "pure" religion. It was from the circles of the "educated" that there originated the "encyclical" to Prior Teller which is attributed to David Friedländer. It offered a readiness to convert, if the confession of a specific Christian dogma were waived and no denial of Judaism (only of its ceremonial) was required.

This undignified and craven approach was properly rejected. But much worse came with the publication in 1803 of Grattenauer's hate-pamphlet *Against the Jews, A Warning to My Christian Fellow-Citizens.* Quickly reaching an edition of 13,000 copies, it described contact with Jews as shameful and pleaded for a renewal of an outward sign of Jewishness, for equality had not improved the Jews. Voices were raised for and against Grattenauer. Among them was a certain Lefrank, whose sympathetic manner was neither then nor later of much success:

> For twenty years the Jew has endeavored to approach the Christian, but how has he been received? How often has he changed his canon law in order to adapt to you—and yet you turn your back on him out of pure humanitarianism. [Dubnow, I, pp. 196 f.]

The Patent of Toleration, with a few later edicts, promulgated by the absolute monarch Joseph II had much more dramatic effects than the timid Prussian reforms, which seldom prevented social respect for or practical tolerance of Jews. Joseph's edicts were intended to be educational and helpful, but they were so hedged by conditions and cost so high a price that not only was their value depleted but they caused much harm. It was intended that the Jews would become useful citizens through training in agriculture, the crafts, and industries; and they were required to adapt to their environment in custom, language, profession, and education. Permitted training in all crafts and commerce, they were not allowed to become masters and could not become full citizens. Normal schools, supposed to be like Christian schools, were established and encouraged, and Jews were admitted to universities and art academies. Among the taxes abolished were the head tax, the double-administration and court tax; the requirements of special attire, noon curfews for Sunday and Holy Day mornings, and for permits to attend places of entertainment were dropped. But the provinces formerly closed remained closed. A few families only were permitted to live in Vienna: in 1804 there were 119 such families, and they paid a total of 18,000 guilders in tribute. In Bohemia and Moravia, the Jews were strictly limited to 14,000 families; only eldest sons could marry. Rights of residence continued to be restricted to the place of original jurisdiction, and permitted sources of income continued according to the fixed norms. As earlier, great sums had to be paid as "protection money," in special taxes, and as contributions. There was censorship of the religious writings of the rabbinate. Rabbis were required to finish both school and university studies in philosophy, the sciences, natural law, and ethics. The Germanizing trend had bitter consequences in Galicia, where marriage licenses were made dependent on proof of passing an examination in German. Military service became obligatory for Jews in Austria in 1788.

V

FROM NAPOLEON TO THE CONGRESS OF VIENNA

Napoleon introduced the French (1791) style of emancipation in France and into the regions—from the left bank of the Rhine to the city of Lübeck—annexed by France in 1811. Comprising full legal and practical equality, it had been curtailed by decree in 1808 which set certain limits on Jewish freedom of movement and freedom to engage in professions, but these restrictions did not apply everywhere. In the Kingdom of Westphalia, for example, the 1807 constitution was to remain the most favorable legal situation achieved by a Jewish minority in a German country for another sixty years. The Napoleonic tenets were in general the same as those of the German emancipationists. What differences appear chiefly reflect the radical quality of a France that could immediately transform laws into practice as opposed to the kind of legal retreats and administrative hindrances common in Germany. "Administrative cheating" was the historian Theodor Mommsen's characterization of this foot-dragging.

It might have been expected that the Rhine Federation would have hastened to follow the Napoleonic reforms. This in general was not the case. Except to abolish the shameful head tax (the last German state to do so), Saxony did nothing. Baden, Würtemberg, and particularly Bavaria lagged greatly behind expectations. Frankfurt, with a huge Jewish population, clung until 1807 to the medieval order of 1616, then permitted itself a French-style equality for a price of 440,000 guilders—and this only after a long series of struggles. In Bavaria, where there had been some improvements, the 1813 Edict on the Jews was a particular disappointment. It confirmed the old system of the "Jewish Protectorate," the restriction of marriage to the oldest son or, in the event of a "vacancy" or an exception, after the payment of 10,000 guilders. It expressly held that "the number of Jewish families, as they are settled at this time, must not be increased in general and, where it is too large, diminished *by and by*." (Dubnow, p. 225.) Austria rarely advanced beyond the limits of the Josephine laws but the application of the rules in Austrian lands was often on the lenient side.

Prussia was the scene of the most interesting developments. After the Peace of Tilsit, the reforms of Stein-Hardenberg called for changes to be made in the legal position of the Jews to bring them into accord with modern circumstances. Under the municipal law of 1808, the rights of citizens were to be independent of one's state of origin, profession, or religion, by which condition "protectorate Jews" under state law gained citizenship rights in the cities. In Berlin in that year, David Friedländer was elected city councilor without pay. Among the leaders of Prussia, there was no longer any question about the desirability of emancipation as a goal. Less clear was whether the state was to be conceived of as a purely legal or an educational institution—whether, in other words, equality would be granted immediately or in stages dependent on educational attainments. The variety of the points of view can be seen in a survey of contemporary documents.

A Councilor Troschel held in 1808:

> If we are reading the signs aright, the moment seems to have arrived when the Prussian legislature is going to follow a sound, strong statecraft that has thrown all prejudice aside. The policing of the Jews and the handling of the problem of toleration are matters too significant to be neglected any longer. . . . It should be decided now: Are Jews unfit to become citizens, or will humanity, reason, and politics dictate that the Jews be conceded the same rights as other inhabitants of the state. [Freund, II, 193.]

A draft bill was prepared in 1809 by Minister of State von Schroetter with the aim of "[undermining] the nationality of the Jews and gradually [leading] them to the point where they no longer form a state within a state." (Freund, II, 228.) In his analysis of this proposal, Wilhelm von Humboldt, at that time a section head for culture and education in the Ministry of the Interior, saw the following reasons as supporting the idea of complete equality:

> Justice: there is nothing in the law to support the denial to the Jew who fulfils all the duties of a Christian the same rights as the Christian. Politics: for those who carry the brunt of the guilt of their brethren and are therefore despised (because of prejudice, because of membership in a certain class), a sudden forward leap is needed. But a gradual reform that permits the continuation of separation in such areas as are not yet reformed will multiply the awareness of the still existing restrictions just because of the newly-won greater liberties.

Humboldt vigorously rejected the concept of the "moral improvement" of the Jews, for—

> if a state wants to be logical in this point, its legislature would have to apportion civic rights according to culture among Christians as well—a fact which, fortunately, has not yet occurred to anybody. . . . When an unnatural state passes into a natural one, there is no jump, certainly not a discernible one; he who becomes a master after having been a servant makes a jump: master and servant are unusual phenomena. But one whose hands are freed after having been shackled, only reaches the point where everyone else already is. [Freund, II, 269.]

Here is classical German humanitarianism making itself heard; Humboldt speaks in a spirit worthy of the tradition of Lessing. But, although he advocates measures that are in themselves mild, he too is in that same line of post-Dohm reformers who, just like the enemies of the Jews (up to the appearance of race hatred of Jews), desired the destruction of Jewry. The "canonic constitution of the Jews, far more political than religious," he felt, is "one of the greatest obstacles to assimilation." Humboldt demanded:

> If you will endeavor to loosen the links between the individual Jewish churches and do not foster a single orthodoxy among the Jews but rather further schisms through a natural and justifiable tolerance, the Jewish hierarchy will fall apart of itself. Individuals will come to realize that theirs is only a ceremonial order but not really a religion, and they will turn toward the Christian faith, driven by the innate human desire for a higher belief. . . . Their conversion, then . . . will become desirable, enjoyable and charitable. [Freund, II, 269.]

One consequence of this fateful suggestion, was the absence of a central Jewish religious organization in Prussia, with the Jews remaining without legal defense in the face of the most infamous accusations of collective guilt (which were preferred to personal charges).

On March 11, 1812, the king signed the Edict of Emancipation submitted by Hardenberg. All Jews residing in the state were recognized as citizens. They were accorded the same civic rights, obligations, and liberties as Christians and were expressly permitted to exercise academic professions and the professions of community administration. The questions of their admission to state administrative posts, their educational institutions, and their religious organization were to be subject to later legislation. Jews were required to take German family names, and all their legal transactions "had to be embodied in the German or another living language." The enthusiasm and gratitude of the Jews was great, and the abolition of rabbinical legislation was accepted without resistance, even of the Orthodox. In a petition concerning reform sent to the king by Friedländer (it was rejected), he wrote:

> Today we have only one fatherland, Prussia, and we must pray for this one only. Our mother tongue is German, and only by the complete and untrammeled introduction of this language can religious services be renewed. [Dubnow, p. 210.]

Young Jews participated with patriotic enthusiasm in the wars of liberation. They suffered dead and wounded. A Jew received the order *Pour le Mérite*, seventy-two received Iron Crosses, and twenty-three were promoted to officer's ranks. The victory, however, little helped Prussian or other German Jews. This was clear before the Congress of Vienna and indubitably clearer afterward, despite the individual efforts on behalf of the Jewish cause by such as Humboldt, Hardenberg, and even Metternich. Early in 1815, Hardenberg dispatched a letter to the Prussian legate to the Hansa cities where, as in Frankfurt, there was haste to re-establish the old conditions of Jewish rightlessness:

> The fate of the Jews . . . in the northern parts of Germany since then [the edict of 1812] must concern the Prussian state; the immorality of which they [the Jews] are accused can only be prolonged by a continuation of the oppression and the hateful exclusion from rights to which as human beings they are entitled. [To continue] this would be to nullify the intention of our ruler, who wants them to participate in all civic rights and duties in order to extinguish any trace of that for which they have been reproached and which arose from just that treatment which expressed contempt and condescension. Moreover, the history of our last war with France has shown them to be worthy of acceptance in the state, to which they have shown great devotion. The young men of the Jewish faith were comrades-at-arms with Christian fellow-citizens, and they have produced examples of true heroism and noble disregard for the dangers of war, just as the other Jewish inhabitants, especially the women, have joined with Christians in every kind of sacrifice. [Baron, p. 88.]

The Jews of the Hansa cites derived little benefit from this, although they were represented in Vienna by an able German lawyer. Expelled from Bremen and Lübeck, in Hamburg they were thrown back to the pitiable conditions of the law of 1710, despite the Senate's averring that the Jews had shown themselves worthy of their civic rights "by most willing efforts for the common weal." The Jews of Frankfurt, whose rights, dearly earned, had already been extensively trimmed, submitted a petition to the Congress to little avail. This dispute was resolved only in 1824—and only in part—when the senate permitted the Jews to form a community as "Israelite citizens" by themselves, but without rights in the administration of the city. The Jews' own administration, on the other hand, was to lay under the supervision of the Senate, and Jews—besides restrictions in trade and commerce—were permitted but fifteen marriages a year for a community of upward of 3,000. This stringent rule was in force for ten years.

In Vienna, a Committee of Five (Austria, Prussia, Hanover, Bavaria, and Würtemberg) was supposed to draft a constitution for the German Bund, including articles concerning the legal standing of the Jews. In the face of resistance from Bavaria, Hanover, and Würtemberg, the more progressive Austria and Prussia continually retreated. The Committee agreed finally on the following formulation:

> Confessors of the Jewish faith insofar as they obligate themselves to the duties of all citizens are granted the same civic rights [as all]; where the constitution of the country is opposed to this reform, the members of the Bund promise to remove to whatever extent is possible, such obstacles. [Baron, p. 152.]

It soon became clear, however, that even this flexible ruling displeased the opponents of the Jews. The final formulation on the rights of the Jews, as it appeared in the constitution of the free cities would remain in force for the Jews. The intriguing and delaying. It declared that:

> The constitutional assembly will deliberate how, and in the most agreeable way, the improvement of the lot of the confessors of the Jewish faith can be achieved in Germany; especially, how civic rights can be achieved and assured to the confessors of this faith against the assurance of their carrying out all the civic duties imposed on them by the

> member states. However, the confessors of this faith will retain the rights which have been conceded to them *by* the individual states of the Bund. [Baron, p. 169.]

Only two weeks earlier, the last sentence had assured the Jews that "the rights which have been conceded to them *in* the individual states" would be retained. The preposition "in" was the subject of vigorous attack. It would have meant that the French-influenced constitutions of various states and of the free cities would remain in force for the Jews. The substitution of "by" changed things substantially. Only what had been conceded voluntarily by a state's administration would be valid. Moreover, on Saxony's insistence, it was now agreed that only unanimous decisions in Vienna would be considered binding. With this, hope for improvement on the Jewish question was forestalled for the future in the Bund assembly. Thus, for example, Hanover instructed its delegate in 1817 to "counteract the incessant attempts of some courts on behalf of the Jews in order to avoid the highly dubious consequences of seeing these exaggerated favors to them spread to our land." (Baron, p. 180.)

VI

REACTION AND THE PRE-MARCH ERA

There was wild anti-Jewish agitation in Germany in the period after the Congress of Vienna. It found expression in such things as the black comedy, *School for Jews.* Berlin historian Friedrich Rühs was an influential anti-Jewish spokesman of the time. In a work published in 1815 (*On the Claims of the Jews to the Rights of German Citizenship*), he declared:

> A foreign people cannot obtain the rights which Germans enjoy partly through being Christians. . . . [It is] forbidden by the very justice of Christians vis-à-vis each other. . . . Everything should be done to induce them [the Jews], in various mild ways, to accept Christianity and through it be led to a true acquisition of German ethnic characteristics and thus to effect the destruction of the Jewish people.

These "mild" ways included a law for foreigners which provided for a tax on Jews, economic supervision, distinguishing signs to be worn on the clothing, and measures against Jewish increase and spread. A professor of philosophy at Heidelberg, a certain Fries, went even further than this in his review of Rühs' work. Arguing from the popular hatred of the Jews—a fact to which the educated were told to attend—Fries advocated the decimation of the Jewish population by marriage reform, expulsion from the villages, restriction of commerce, and other restrictions. Friedrich Jahn would permit no Jew to join his *Turnverein* and announced that "Poles, Frenchmen, priests, junkers, and Jews are Germany's affliction." (Sterling, p. 164.) University fraternities were at first similarly hostile.

Whereas Rühs opposed violent measures and advocated leaving the human rights of Jews unimpaired, more drastic proposals are to be found in the *Judenspiegel* ("The Jewish Mirror") of 1819, published by Hartwig Hundt-Radowsky and prohibited in Prussia. He advised sending the Jews to work in the mines or their sale to England for work in her colonies. The men should be emasculated and the women sent to brothels. "The best way, however, would be to clear the whole country of this vermin by destroying them totally or, as Pharaoh did, expelling them from the country." In this view, the murder of a Jew was neither a sin nor a crime. It was a "misdemeanor."

The Jews themselves protested only meekly against the flood of these defamations. Christians who took the part of the Jews usually did so with specific reservations. Professor Alexander Lips of Erlangen, for example, saw the importance of Jewish equality to achieving other, more general goods, but he was far from satisfied with the Jews as people. He said that they needed several generations of education before they could be considered equals. Still, he counseled the German people sincerely to take heed that "we infect our children with hatred of the Jew and then nourish it busily at a later age, but we do not attack the reasons that generate this need in us, the hidden sources within us, our own hatred and our own will to be separate." (Elbogen, p. 211.) Lips feared that unchecked slanders against the Jews would unleash catastrophe. It was, indeed, to come very soon. Students blamed both Metternich and the House of Rothschild for the notorious Karlsbad decisions; their ranks swollen with other discontented citizens, the student movement against these reactionary measures led to riots against the Jews in 1819. The following proclamation of that time breathes the spirit of pure hatred:

> Brethren in Christ! Rise, meet, and arm yourselves with courage and strength against the enemies of the faith: the time has come to suppress the generation of Christ-killers that they not become rulers over you and your children, for the Jewish hordes are raising their heads in triumph. . . . Down with them, before they crucify our priests, defile our sanctuaries, and destroy our temples: we still have power over them . . . let us now carry out their judgment on us against them. . . . Arise all those who are baptized . . . a most sacred thing is at stake! Those Jews who are living among us and who are increasing like locusts. . . . We call for revenge against them, and our battlecry will be "Hepp! Hepp! Hepp! Death and destruction to all the Jews! You must flee or you will die." [Sterling, p. 189.]

Impelled by such writings, there was unrest in many cities: robbing, looting, physical abuse, murder. Würzburg, where it had begun, was the chief site of the virulence. There, instead of punishing the guilty, four hundred Jews were expelled from the city. It is small wonder that the cause of emancipation was set back in this period.

Decrees to nullify the rights of Jews were promulgated in

Prussia beginning with the year 1816. There had been no less than thirty-five different laws according rights to Jews, their number varying somewhat in relation to the conditions of reconquest and annexation. In the original Tilsit countries, the law of 1812 was severely trimmed but not abolished. The petitions of Jewish war widows for pensions were denied on grounds of the religion of the deceased. In the military, rank above corporal was closed to Jews. Jewish eligibility for municipal or state posts was denied or revoked. The state posts promised to winners of the Iron Cross were denied to Jewish medal holders. Von Kircheisen, Minister of Justice, held that "the suspicion of diminished morality is not invalidated by a temporary show of valor." (Elbogen, p. 204.) A spokesman for the Ministry of Finance declared:

> It would be preferable to have no Jews in the country. But since we must tolerate those that are here, we should unfailingly attempt to render them harmless. Conversion of Jews to Christianity should be made easier; in this manner the Jew will attain all his civic rights. As long as a Jew remains a Jew, however, he cannot hold a position in the government where, representing the state, he would be in a position to rule over Christian citizens. [Dubnow, II, 37.]

Apostasy, which men like Börne and Heine accepted, was thus encouraged. Between 1812 and 1845 in Prussia, there were 3,370 baptisms of Jewish converts. Personal conviction was probably seldom a motive.

Prussian conditions were not as bad as those in most other German states. In Saxony the situation was still on the level of the medieval. Immigration and freedom of movement were prohibited to Jews, who were confined to Dresden and Leipzig. The king's own edict was necessary in 1834 to permit a tailor to take on a Jewish apprentice. With a ratio of 1,900

Christian inhabitants to each Jew, the crafts petitioned for "protection against Jewry."

The Bavarian situation is revealed in the unsuccessful petition prepared and presented by several Jewish communities to the diet in 1831:

> We 50,000 inhabitants of the kingdom who share the duties and taxes with our fellow Christian inhabitants and fulfil the very same obligations still have not obtained any civic rights and . . . are still lacking in the most basic human rights. . . . [We] sigh under the heavy pressure of the unjust exceptional laws, the abolition or alteration of which has been solemnly promised for the last twelve years and has been requested often and urgently from the state government. It is an unvarying and inviolable human right: to have a fatherland, freely to employ one's abilities of body and mind, to hold property, to settle, to marry, to raise and educate one's children and in turn leave them a fatherland, a proper place of their own, and the assured possession and employment of these human rights. But when there are laws that aim to limit families, to prohibit offspring, to restrict settlement to certain places in certain numbers, there our children have no fatherland, no property, no gainful employment. They are condemned to celibacy and to do without the rights of fathers and of men, and thus to decline physically and morally. [Dubnow, II, 62.]

These were the conditions, too, in Austria, where little progress was made in the pre-March era beyond the Josephine legislation. The change in Austria, as everywhere else, was in a strengthening of the Jewish determination to assimilate by conversion, a rise in general Jewish culture, and the economic development of the Jewish upper classes. Talented converts were favored and in nearly every profession occupied important positions. There was a considerable emigration of Jews to America. The atmosphere began to improve for the Jews in general only after 1831, when the question began to be viewed with noticeably more objectivity. We find in an essay in the review *Deutscher Horizont* for 1831: "Hatred of Jews begins where sound reason leaves off. The reader can be sure that whenever the word 'Jew' is spat out, the speaker has either not come into his right mind or has left it behind." (Sterling, p. 55.)

Widespread as confusion was at this time among Jews, who were experiencing the breakdown of tradition without the concomitant growth of new forms, there now came upon the scene the uniquely courageous and articulate defender of the Jews, Gabriel Riesser. A lawyer and by avocation a politician, Riesser demanded equality for the Jews on humanitarian grounds and defended an idealistic, but not a cynical, kind of assimilation. His views were spelled out in numerous articles from 1830 on. When Karl Steckfuss, a Prussian government councilor, pronounced himself in favor of an arrangement by which rich and well-educated Jews might receive citizenship with some restrictions, for their special merits, while the other Jews, limited in their elementary rights, were to become patronage subjects, Riesser fought the proposal so decisively that the distinction between "naturalized Jews" and "those unfit for naturalization" was made only in the province of Posen, where in 1816 only eight of 52,000 Jewish inhabitants were citizens. It would be wrong, however, to leave Steckfuss with the label of an enemy of the Jews, for in 1844 he stood for unconditional and unrestricted emancipation, although it is clear that he had been affected in 1833 by the opinions then prevailing. At that time he had believed that if Jews would only choose to join the Christian state society and deny their separate existence and their national characteristics, "there would be only German citizens of the Mosaic faith, but no Jewish nation such as is still trying to impose itself as separate from the German nation and thus makes it quite clear that it does not want to blend with us in customs and thought." To Steckfuss, the unassimilated Jew was a difficult foreigner whose unpleasant appearance, different language and customs make him "hated by the masses, who cannot understand the differences, and [create] a climate of opinion which affects every other respectable class [of assimilated Jews] equally hard." (Mieses, p. 568.)

Riesser's arguments against these accusations are remarkable. They are to be found in his *Views on the Conditions of Jewish Subjects of the Prussian Monarch,"* 1834:

> The constant identification of religion with outward advantage, the everyday events in Prussia that show conversion to be the condition of achieving citizenship status, must in the end lead to the externalization of religion, its profession becoming a civic act with no relationship to truth or conviction. By far the greater number of the Jews who devoted themselves to the sciences in the hope of state preferment on the basis of the law of 1812 have converted only after long struggles and vain attempts to effect the application of the law. Consequent to this, they have achieved successful careers in the fields of academic teaching as well as in many branches of local government and administration. Very few of them had the means to live independently for arts and letters, to seek abroad the distinction and activity denied them at home, or, having finished their studies, to enter another career, such as commerce, agriculture, or manufacturing; many of them—and some who were extremely gifted in mind and attainments—

> contented themselves with modest positions of teaching in private schools for Jewish boys or with establishing such schools—a very useful enterprise, but one far below their merit. Hardly a tenth of all the scientists of Jewish families since 1812 have been saved for Jewry. [Riesser, III, 7.]

In this Riesser sketches the portrait of the assimilated Jews, or those who were willing to assimilate, and who desired only the permission to keep a special religious position vis-à-vis their state and society. But state and society demanded that a citizen combine German nationality with the Christian religion, and this demand was maintained until the question of Jewish assimilation was no longer viable. For in the meantime the hatred of Jews became thoroughly secularized, and Germanized Jews were to be no part of the German ethnic community. Riesser, like many of Dohm's disciples after him up to the catastrophe itself, thought it correct to hold that the Jews were but a religious community within the German nation and, on that basis, were entitled to be full-fledged Germans. Assimilationist Jews did not think of themselves as Jewish nationals. They were Germans, and their determination to be such involved no intellectual denial. They had been raised as Germans.

VII

JEWISH WAYS FROM MENDELSSOHN TO RIESSER

How did the Jews of Germany adjust to conditions in the period of the start of emancipation? The conditions themselves could not have remained unchanged, for in Mendelssohn's time the economic, cultural, and social facts of Jewish life were already outmoded.

In matters of social development, it is usually the elite of a group that recognizes the direction of new growth, and the great majority is inclined to stay with the tradition, whether difficult or not, and this attitude is slow to be overcome. Where this is not the case, there must be immense compelling forces or insupportable conditions to change the will of the masses. Both possibilities have relevance to the situation at the beginning of Jewish emancipation; either may well account for the astonishing development that occurred in the brief span of three generations. Another way to view this is through the group's composite profile, a nearly indefinable amalgamation of progressive and reactionary tendencies within the group. We will briefly review only the most important of these.

Mendelssohn had written in 1782: "Thanks to Almighty

Providence, which has permitted me to live to this day in which human rights are beginning to be thought of in their fulness." (Mendelssohn, III, 179.) Since this was written when nothing had changed in Jewish conditions since the Josephine reforms, it can signify only Mendelssohn's hope and the general tenor of the times. Mendelssohn, moreover, was the first Jew to deny the national distinction between German and Jew. This is clear in his reply to a critic of Dohm:

> Instead of using the expression "Christians and Jews," Mr. Michaelis is continually served by "Germans and Jews." He refuses to recognize that the difference is in religion only and prefers to have us regarded as foreigners who must accept the conditions laid down to them by the owners of the land. . . . Would it not be to the best interests of mankind and culture to forget about this difference? [Mendelssohn, III, 367.]

The implication of this is that national differences are artificial or outdated, a view that continued to be that of Mendelssohn's disciples, although they did not usually advance it with a dignity equal to their master's.

As an emancipationist and deist, Mendelssohn saw no conflict between the teachings of Judaism and of reason; he considered, however, that Jewish revelation supported and assured the group existence of the Jews. Here he spoke as an orthodox, tradition-bound Jew. The next generation of "progressives"—to use a relative term which may be dangerous in this connection—saw things differently. As they became more "German," they became more like the Germans in religion as well: this is what had been asked of them. Anything that might set them apart—let it be the Law of Moses—had to be suppressed. As Friedländer said: "Special nationality, special food laws, special education—all this has to give way to the full acceptance of the state and the fulfillment of the duties of citizenship—except the faith of Israel and its ritual manifestation." Because the spokesmen of the requisite reforms lived in Protestant cities, these reforms tended to bring Protestant forms of worship into Jewish rites. Prayers were said to the accompaniment of German-singing choirs; many prayers were spoken in German; others, especially those of a nationalistic character, were omitted; organ music was introduced; there was preaching in German; and confirmations of both boys and girls were celebrated.

When these innovations encountered violent opposition, this in turn aroused the reformers to new affirmations of the desirability of Jewish cultural and social assimilation, nearly always accompanied by the specific denial of the nationality of Jews. While the reformers began their work without overall plan, under the influence of the German example they tried to formulate their proposals as a system. This approach is reflected in the title of the periodical brought out under the editorship of the radical rabbi, Abraham Geiger, in 1835. It was called the *Scientific Review for Jewish Theology*. Geiger proposed "science, not religion" as the new basis of Jewish life, Judaism now being understood not as a life teaching but as a theology and a religion. In 1844, the "Reformgenossenschaft" declared:

> We can no longer truly pray with our mouth for a kingdom of a Messiah here and now, which would take us away from the fatherland to which we are greatly devoted, to take us away as if from a foreign country to lead us to the homeland of our forefathers. We can no longer recognize as unchangeable a code which insists that Jews

> give a rigid adherence to forms which originated in ancient times forever gone. [Kobler, II, 79.]

With this, religion entered the service of emancipation and Germanization.

Orthodox circles rallied and found their first widely popular speaker in the figure of Rabbi Samson Raphael Hirsch. He denied that the Jews of pre-Messianic times constituted a nation, but he saw Jewish duty as adherence to tradition; yet in this he saw no obstacle to assimilation. This integration of orthodoxy to a political view was put forward in 1839:

> People may stunt your right to be a human being and to develop a just human life on the soil which bore you but you (must) never lose sight of your duty, be just to yourself, to the duty which God asks of you: *Faith to the sovereign and the country and the promotion of salvation wherever and whenever you can.* [Hirsch, *Chorev.*]

Jewish intellectuals rarely professed themselves part of a Jewish people with desires for emancipation during the pre-March years. At this time, such persons could rarely be found outside Posen, West Prussia, or Upper Silesia. In general, the intellectuals' attitude—bespeaking little consciousness of tradition—involved the profession of only a religion as such. A voice of the minority is heard in the letters of Israel Deutsch, Rabbi of Beuthen:

> In recent times, Jews and non-Jews have been talking at length about assimilation. . . . As persons and as citizens of the state and the world, we can come close to each other and love each other, but as a people we must remain separated on the outside until the time that it pleases Providence to abolish all differences of faith inside and outside. . . . Maturity for emancipation! This is something which I

> do not find lacking at all. It appears that the Negroes are ripe for emancipation in the eyes of every true humanitarian—and the Jews are not? . . . Our enemies . . . surely know no other kind of maturity than baptism. [Kobler, II, 99, 102.]

As has been seen, this view truly characterizes the desire of most of the Jewish emancipators. But in the rush to attain equality, which had been achieved in cultural matters in Berlin while the legal position of Jews lagged far behind (until the Hardenberg Edict and the quick reaction to it), conversion beckoned. Every degree of acceptance played a role here —true conviction, the indifference to undergoing a merely necessary formality, and the cynicism of a Heine, who called baptism a "ticket to enter European culture." The tragedy of these early assimilationists, however, can be seen in the fact that three of Mendelssohn's four children converted, and all his grandchildren were Christians. Rachel Varnhagen, one of the most important figures in this circle, a woman deeply attached to Germany, could not close her eyes to the situation:

> In my fantasies I see a supernatural being which has a dagger poised to thrust into my heart . . . saying: "Have compassion, see the world as only a few see it, be great and noble, and I cannot deny you an eternal mind." But one command I forgot: "Be a Jewess!" and now my whole life is nothing but the ebbing away of my life blood. [Varnhagen, *Briefwechsel Rahel-Veit*, p. 79.]

On her deathbed, she confessed that

> In this country I am a refugee from Palestine and Egypt, and I find help, care, and love only in you! I think about my origins with elation, and of the historical connections

> between the most ancient human concerns and memories with the newest shape of things in the furthest reaches of time and space. The bane of my existence, the cause of the greatest sorrow and unhappiness for me—having been born a Jew—I would not want to miss now for anything. [Varnhagen, Rahel, I, 43.]

A society for the culture and science of Judaism was formed in Berlin in 1819 by several young Jewish intellectuals. Young Heine was a member. Five years later, the society no longer existed. Its aim had not only failed to arouse sufficient interest, but most of its membership had sought baptism. Of them all, there remained as a Jew only the great Leopold Zunz, the man who founded modern Judaism and whose work is at the level of Jacob Grimm's but received the scant attention given all Jewish historical works during the era of emancipation. In a letter of 1825, his despair at the spiritual condition of the Jews is evident:

> The Jews and the Judaism which we aim to reconstruct are torn apart, the victims of barbers, fools, money-changers, idiots, and *parnassim* [community elders]. Time and time will pass and this generation will be unchanged: riven, spilling over into the Christian religion out of need, without backbone or principle, part still in the old mire, barely vegetating, pushed aside by Europe. . . . I have arrived at such a pass that I believe no longer in a reform for the Jews; this illusion should be exorcised. . . . The only thing which survives immortally from this *mabbul* [the great flood] is the "science of Judaism," for it still lives, although not a finger has been raised for it in centuries. I confess that, next to my trust in God's justice, occupation with this science is my consolation and my only support. [Dubnow, II, 115.]

Thus, Judaism became a science rather than a life teaching, although it was a living science for Zunz. Yet a science of any kind cannot form the life of a group. Ever since the beginning of the eighteenth century, the Jewish group had lost its form —whether the form is considered positive or negative is incidental—it had been divided, fallen apart, and had existed in a kind of transitional state, but without clear goal. Direction was finally pointed out by Gabriel Riesser (1806–63). Grandson of an immigrant rabbi from Lithuania who had rejected the Chassidic mysticism of his native land as he had the enlightened views of Mendelssohn, Riesser was neither a rabbi nor a theologian. He became a jurist and politician and the first Jewish politician to consider himself wholly a German and yet to support the cause of the Jews fearlessly when it was required. He, who as a child had suffered expulsion from Lübeck and who was later denied any kind of lectureship and admission to the bar, became a fighter for the whole Jewish group, using truth as his only weapon. These quotations from his polemics show the distance between the first and third generations of Jews who voluntarily assimilated and "who [did] not want to be different from their fellow citizens except in their . . . inherited or chosen way of worship."

> To the charge that we are unbelievers cast out by God, we reply that we believe in a God who casts out none of his children; but would a German call us, Germans, foreigners, we would be without a home and a fatherland. . . . It is as inhuman as it is insane to reproach us with the fact that our forefathers immigrated here a hundred or a thousand years ago; *we are not immigrants, but were born here and therefore have no right to any other home; either we are Germans or we are homeless. . . . He who contests my right to my German fatherland, contests my right to my*

> *own thoughts, my sentiments, the language I am speaking, and the air I breathe; therefore I must defend myself against him as I would against a murderer. Lucky that I can do this at least in my own German language, which is more loving than her children and takes care of me in a motherly way; she will not deny me the most potent arms in this struggle.* [Riesser, IV, 303.]

Riesser spoke for many of the best young Jews of the time. The words of the young writer, Berthold Auerbach, are indicative:

> We rely upon the living customs of the nation; we respect German customs and German compassion. I live in the happy and confident conviction that I express the ideas of the entire generation of young Jews when I add: Put us to the acid test of danger. You will find us clean of the residues of egoism and the indecency of over-refinement. Allow us the fatherland to which we belong by birth, custom, and love, and we shall gladly lay down our lives and possessions on its altar. Let us forget the dark wall of division between us; spare us the hurtful need to oppose you because you so often place your patriotic efforts side by side with the demon of Jewish hatred. [Geiger, p. 239.]

VIII

1848

The events of 1848 brought the Jews close—only close—to the fulfilment of great expectations. Their fate, however, was more deeply influenced by the nature of the three major political trends of those times—trends which preceded the Revolution and continued in effect afterward. The 1847 debates in the United Diet of Prussia saw the delegates argue for seven days over a draft law proposing the emancipation of the Jews with respect to the civil (but not the public) law, an emancipation to take effect in a series of stages. All political tendencies—conservative, liberal, and radical—including those well disposed toward the Jews, hoped for the blending of the Jews and their surroundings, a good tantamount to the dissolution of the Jewish group. This kind of emancipation seems to have been in the air all through the twenty-five years that antedated the founding of the Second Empire; from 1843 on, many provincial diets, in the Rhineland especially, pronounced themselves in favor of emancipation. The prevailing three general viewpoints can be elucidated through the speeches of the United Diet of 1847, preserved in the *Complete Debates of the First United Prussian Diet* con-

cerning the Question of the Emancipation of the Jews.

We will attend first to the conservatives. Minister von Thile considered it

> irreconcilable with Christendom, to grant the Jews any rights in government. For they would then be expected to take part either in the administration or the creation of laws whose essence is permeated with the Christian spirit. These demands must cause a conflict of conscience insofar as the Jew maintains his Old Testament point of view in matters of faith.

Thile spoke in favor of a complete emancipation to be granted only if "the Jews give up their separate and divisive law." To him it was inescapably clear that "the Jew cannot have another fatherland than the one anchored in his belief: Zion is the fatherland of the Jews." Deputy von Manteuffel, stressing the "still persisting distance between Jewish believers and the Christian customs of the state," wondered why "the Christian state should take the first step vis-à-vis the Jews." Prince Radziwill was more blunt: "The doors are open all the time to complete emancipation. If they convert and assume Christianity, they will be our brothers in every way and will have civic and political rights."

The youthful eloquence of Bismarck, if ebullient, is nonetheless indicative of his later views:

> I think it is correct to say that a state is Christian if it has made its task the realization of the teachings of Christianity. . . . I am not an enemy of the Jews. Under certain conditions, I can even love them. I concede every right to them, except the right to take a governmental position in a Christian state. . . . Should I imagine myself faced by a Jewish representative, whom I must obey, of his holy majesty, the king, I must confess I would feel deeply

> crushed and depressed; the joy and upright honor that sustain me in fulfilling my duties toward the state would completely abandon me.

Here, even Bismarck shared the common sentiment: "I share this feeling with the masses of the common people, and I am not ashamed of being in this company."

While the liberals cast their votes for complete emancipation, they also made plain what they expected of the Jews. Count Renard: "It would be illogical to permit the Jews to remain in the strict isolation into which they were forced by previous legislation. . . . The Jews must accept the hand being offered them; they may keep their faith, but they must put superstition and heresy away." What heresy or superstition is intended, if not the Jewish faith itself? Count York: "I hope the Jews become Christians. Experience teaches us that emancipation is the best means toward this end."

The radical attitude was, above all, critical of society. It was because society barred the Jews from most of the other liberal professions that there had developed a preponderance of Jews in the field of journalism, for example, which the radical spokesman Mewissen hardly approved:

> As one consequence of the Jewish inclination toward the work of the mind and research, and probably as a consequence of the pressure exerted against the Jews, they have fallen prey to a spirit of hate, of bitter scorn . . . which is having an acid and poisonous influence on present views. As we look around, we find more and more of journalism in the hands of the Jews; and we find that the literature of despair, the literature of *Weltschmerz*, has primarily been fostered by the Jews among us.

On the Jewish side, Jews took part in the street fighting in Berlin, Vienna, and other cities during the Revolution itself.

They were among the defenders of the castle in Berlin. Rabbis and priests officiated together for the first time over the bodies of fallen fighters. Even then, however, there were in Baden, Bavaria, and Hamburg, riots of the lower classes against the Jews. Nonetheless, Jews had hopes of unrestricted equality, and they argued chiefly with the tools afforded by the liberals. Soliman von Hönigsberg of Propue, thus, took a position which has a very modern ring:

> If any immigrant may become a citizen, if an emigrant who has expressed his intent to emigrate loses no rights up to emigration itself, why is the Jew treated as a foreigner? . . . Origin, blood, the purely physical can never form the basis of decisions in civil or constitutional law.

The tendency among the Jews was to take a position of complete identification with the German state. Normally, however, this did not go quite to the lengths of a statement by Rabbi Abraham Geiger in a letter of 1840: "It is more important to me that the Jews of Prussia can become druggists and jurists than that all the Jews of Asia and Africa, in whose fate I am interested as a human being, have or have not achieved salvation."

Among the delegates to the Frankfurt National Assembly, there were four Jews, including Riesser, reporter for the committee on constitutional reform and later elected vice-president of the assembly by a great majority. If we include converted Jews in the tally (a practice that was disapproved at the time) we have the astonishingly high total of seventeen Jewish deputies, including the lawyer Eduard Simson, elected president of the assembly. He led the delegation, which included Riesser, to offer the imperial crown to Frederick William IV of Prussia. On August 19, the "basic rights of the German people" (as expressed in Paragraph 13: "The exercise of civic or constitutional rights is in no way hindered or restricted by religious creed. The citizen's duties are in no way impaired by religious creed") were debated. Deputy Mohl proposed an amendment: "The peculiar conditions of the Israelite ethnic group are subject to special legislation that may be requested by the Reich. The Israelite members of the German state are granted active and passive voting rights." (Dubnow, II, 322.) This odd proposal, which granted parliamentary rights while it denied equality, like every other proposal in Germany since 1812, was defended by the familiar argument, advanced here by Mohl: The emancipation of the separate Jewish ethnic group should not occur before its adoption of true German attitudes. Riesser replied to Mohl:

> I have the privilege to appear before you in the name of a class which has been oppressed through centuries, a class to which I belong by birth and continue to belong—though my personal religious conviction is not under discussion here—*by dint of the principle of honor which made me scorn the acquisition, by means of a change in religion, of rights so insolently denied me*. . . . The honorable previous speaker has couched his proposal within an untruth. He wants to exempt by exceptional law the Israelite *ethnic group* from the equal application of the laws. You have just solemnly assured all non-German-speaking ethnic groups in Germany of equality before the law, equality of rights, and equality in everything which makes Germany dear to the Germans. Should we Jews, then, consider it our misfortune that we speak German? . . . Shall history say of you that you desired to appease those powerful ones who might harm Germany, that you could muster none but mild expressions in the face of these threats while,

toward a weak religious grouping which wanted nothing as citizens than to blend as Germans, you gave harsh treatment? You must judge us as you would any other mass of people—according to those who are articulate and vividly sensitive and who have a clear recognition of their condition. This is a class that refuses the nationality tagged on to them by their enemies; it is a class that thinks and feels as Germans. You propose an exceptional law for these, while you demand the abolition of exceptional laws, and you expect this law, these statutes, to heal the wounds of society? . . .

The previous speaker would grant us political rights, but this permission is of very recent date. I myself have lived under conditions of the most dire oppression, and *until a short time ago I could not even have been hired as a night watchman in my home town.* I might consider it a work—or rather a wonder—of justice and freedom that I am here able to defend before you a matter of high justice and equality *without having embraced Christianity.* It is because of this that I live in the firm conviction that the good has already triumphed, despite the last seethings of ill will on several sides. . . . I must admit that under the present state of oppression the Jews have not yet acquired the highest spirit of patriotism. *But the Jews will become ever more enthusiastic and patriotic followers of Germany under a just law. The Jews will be Germans among the Germans.* Have confidence in the power of the law, the power of a unified law, and in the great fate of Germany. Do not allow yourselves to believe that exceptional laws can be passed without damaging the whole delicate fabric of the system of liberty, without sowing the seed of destruction. You have been asked to abandon a part of the German people to intolerance and hatred. This, gentlemen, you will never do. [Riesser, III, 565.]

After Riesser's speech, Mohl's proposal was rejected with near unanimity. But "the basic laws of the German people" did not become official, and the national assembly dispersed in 1849. Despite many setbacks, however, the situation of the Jews did improve in the sense of the Frankfurt declaration. The situation was as the great historian Simon Dubnow, summed it up:

> Formally, constitutionally-guaranteed equality of the Jews was in force in 1848 in nearly all of the individual German states, even in such reactionary ones as Saxony and Mecklenburg. *De jure*, Jewish slavery had been done away with in the free cities of Hamburg and Frankfurt. Actually, however, during the first period following the Revolution, Jews enjoyed parliamentary suffrage only, the other restrictions on them remaining until they might be abolished by ordinary legislation. Thus it came about that the Jewish inhabitants of the country were denied their most inalienable rights, while Jewish deputies were full-fledged members of parliament. [Dubnow, II, 325.]

It is hard to imagine today the enthusiastic German nationalism of the Jews of that time. Although denied the most elementary rights in Schleswig-Holstein, Jews even volunteered for the war of liberation there. Prussia's restrictive policy against Jews in Posen did not detain Jews from unreservedly taking the part of Prussia during the Polish revolution. On the question of the Reich, Jews largely took the side of Prussia. A good deal of evidence of the great enthusiasm of the Jews has survived. We have for instance the letter of the jurist Levin Goldschmidt to his parents in 1848: "Much that we asked for only last year has now been obtained. Now the Jew, too, can choose his way according to his inclination and his talents; he no longer needs to court fortune through the abnegation of his faith." (Kobler, II, 41.) Goldschmidt's optimism was not really justified; he himself did not succeed in obtaining the position at a Prussian university that he sought and ended up at Heidelberg instead.

Just as assimilation in the political, social, and cultural spheres spread with virtually no opposition from Posen to Karlsruhe, from Hamburg to Vienna, thus the reform spirit in the religious sphere had spread through most of the provincial Jewish communities. In Worms it was announced in 1848: "We must . . . no longer pray in a dead language when words and sounds of our German tongue are equally meaningful and charming and therefore solely apt to elevate us toward our Creator." (Kobler, II, 41.)

IX

SETBACKS AND PROGRESS

The era between the bourgeois revolution and the founding of the North German Federation was for the Jews of Germany a period of general advancement toward complete emancipation marked by a number of setbacks. Analysis reveals these counter-movements to have been the results of rear-guard action by the old conservatives, who had finally retreated before the onslaught of a liberalism no longer inimical toward the Jews. The period bore a resemblance to the first easing of the conditions of the Jews at the beginning of the century, when a small upper stratum of Jews were recognized as culturally and socially the equal of Christians. Now in addition to social equality, the Jews achieved economic equality on the basis of legal emancipation, which benefited a greater number of Jews. There were still very powerful enemies of the Jews, as there had been in 1800—they were never quite silenced in Germany—but they did not exercise so much influence as heretofore on the makers of public opinion. Tragically, however, for the emancipation of the Jews of Germany, the decisive victories—1812 and 1869—were met by the challenges of an enemy camp, which, in the first instance, fought for nearly fifty years before petering out. In the second, it culminated in the abolition of emancipation and the destruction of the Jews.

Let us now look more closely at the situation of German Jewry in the years following the Revolution. Old-style orthodoxy had nearly vanished among the Jews of Germany and the western provinces of Austria. The Jewish way of life had accommodated itself to that of the rest of the population even in matters of religious rites. By mid-century, therefore, assimilation with and accommodation to the secularized life of Germany was no problem. There was no need to strive to achieve assimilation; assimilation had been achieved. The larger portion of Jewry was liberal, the remainder Neo-Orthodox. Knowledge of the Jewish cultural tradition and Jewish history was often meager or lacking altogether. German culture was generally much better known. The distribution, however, of Jews in the professions was unbalanced. For reasons arising from historical and contemporary circumstances, a normal distribution was never reached, nor was it ever in the realm of possibility. While such an imbalance may have created some problems, these in no way had the significance attributed to them by enemies of the Jews. The opposition was intent only on feeding tensions and exploiting weaknesses for tactical benefit, rather than on resolving problems in any reasonable manner.

When the Bundestag in 1851 voided the "basic rights," the individual states considered themselves no longer bound to uphold the concessions of 1848, and they returned to their more or less reactionary constitutions. Not even the most reactionary states, however, could re-establish the stodgy atmosphere of pre-1848, despite the fact that some found it unnecessary to cancel the edict of Frankfurt before voiding promises or countermanding earlier orders of toleration. The idea of a Christian state again prevailed in Prussia, as it had in the pre-March era; it was expressly formulated by the conservative politician, Friedrich Julius Stahl, a Jewish convert, in 1847: "The only hindrance to the political equality of the Jews . . . is the Christian character of the state." (Stahl.) The revised constitution of 1851 carried forward in its Article 12 the declaration of the draft of 1848: equal civic and constitutional rights, without respect to religion. But the intent of Article 12 was absolutely canceled by Article 14: "The Christian religion is the basis for all the institutions of the state which are connected with the exercise of religion." Consequently, Jews could not be civil servants, judges, teachers, or lawyers. The practice was eased under the regency of the future King William I, although the restrictions on Jews in administrative posts were kept up. Jews were admitted to the bar, and there were other concessions. In parliament there were three Jewish deputies, and Jews held honorary posts in various municipalities.

But equality in law was yet to be attained. Official prejudice in Prussia against the Jews was the subject of two 1860 pamphlets by Riesser. That year, Levin Goldschmidt, the renowned jurist who had unsuccessfully competed for a post in Prussia, wrote in a letter accepting his appointment as extraordinary professor at Heidelberg that "the newest decree of the Ministry of Culture concerning the chances for the appointment of Jews to posts in education have completely dashed my hopes for Prussia." (Kobler, II, 44.) The new legal opportunities that arose with the accession of new territories in 1864 and 1866, as had happened after 1813, were shortlived. At the same time, despite the failure to reach full emancipatory status, the Jews viewed the rising state of

Prussia with overwhelming sympathy. This is the tenor of a work by the Jewish philosopher—one of the rare Jewish public figures of his time who considered himself intellectually and religiously a Jew—Moritz Lazarus; it was entitled *On the Ethical Justification of Prussia as Part of Germany* (1850). Sympathy for the Jews was widespread among conservative Prussians, despite there having been no change in the situation of the Jews. In a personal letter from the diplomat Josias von Bunsen to the scholar Jacob Bernays, in which von Bunsen counsels Bernays to convert, we find:

> Your stand with respect to tradition is the same as mine—that is [you take] the point of view of world history. The difference is that I am following the current of history, and you are going counter to it. The loss of nationality is difficult. But the denial of one's consciousness of history is even more difficult, for it is hopeless. [Fraenkel, p. 52.]

From the fact of his culture being younger than that of the Jew and far superior to it in point of power, the Christian was arguing on Hegelian premises that the superior power was historically determined. History had made an unfavorable judgment on the Jews.

In Austria there had been no changes in the period between the Josephine legislation and 1848; in 1849, however, the new constitution decreed complete emancipation. Never entirely realized, emancipation was revoked with the constitution in 1851, when the Jews again became the subject of special legislation. The prohibition on land ownership was reinstated, but without retroactive force; freedom of movement was again restricted; the special oath for Jews reintroduced; and certain professions were ruled out for Jews. In the Czech and Polish areas of the empire, the Jews found themselves caught in the struggle between the nationalities and the Germans. In Hungary, the government relied on education to Germanize the Jews. From 1860 on, the Jewish position in Hungary improved markedly and in 1867 the fundamental law declared unrestricted emancipation: "Before the law all citizens are equal, and all citizens have access to public office; the enjoyment of civic and political rights is independent of religious denomination." The decree was largely put into practice, and the Jewish situation was better in Hungary than in any other German land.

In Baden, emancipation had been progressing slowly since the time of Napoleon. Despite the proclamation of emancipation, freedom of movement had remained under restrictions, as did settlement rights and the rights to engage in various professions and types of commerce. Settlement was impermissible in Constance, Baden-Baden, and Offenburg. Baden-Baden refused permission in 1861 to a Jew who wished to settle. Constitutional emancipation preceded emancipation under municipal laws, unlike the situation in Prussia. The process was completed only in 1862. Despite protests from the estates, Würtemberg did not restrict the legal position of the Jews when the Frankfurt "basic rights" were voided. In 1861, political rights were granted, followed by the granting of civic rights in 1864, with only a single vote in opposition.

The Bavarian government had withstood the pressure of 1848 for emancipation and had only promised "improvements." During the deliberations of the second house of the Reichsrat on the Jewish question in 1850, six hundred anti-Jewish petitions were received with 80,000 signatures. The petitions had been gathered and circulated by priests, ultramontanes, and civil servants. Emancipation was defeated, and in the next year the restrictive conditions of 1813 were virtually reinstated. Specifically, there were restrictions on the number of Jews in the population and on the number of Jewish marriages. One consequence of this reaction was the continuation of the Bavarian-Jewish emigration to the United States that had been going on for decades. There was progress, however, in Nuremberg, where Jews—expelled since 1499—were legally admitted and where in 1861 family restrictions were altogether abolished. While settlement and economic restrictions were also eased, complete emancipation came only with the Reich's adoption of the law of 1872. An exception to the general pattern of Bavarian politics, Jews were allowed to be officers in the Landwehr. Karl Obermeyer, for example, became a colonel in 1863, the highest rank until then obtained by a Jewish officer. This anomalous Bavarian practice was shared by Austria but by no other future part of the Second Empire. Nor did it last very long in Bavaria.

While equality continued as law in Saxony after the Revolution, the real conditions of Saxony were much like those of Bavaria. Under pressure from the merchants of Leipzig and Dresden, the parliament meekly consented in 1852 to restricting Jewish rights. Jewish settlement in these cities was forbidden as late as 1867, when Jews settled in Chemnitz and Plauen, with full emancipation coming in 1868. Hessen-Kassel had been particularly reactionary: there the equality decreed in 1833 was revoked and citizenship was made to depend upon one's confession of Christianity. Hamburg was one of the few sovereign territories to realize emancipation with any speed. Riesser, the first Jewish judge, became a member of the supreme court in 1860 and vice-president of the "Burgerschaft" the same year. In the other countries during the period 1848–68, emancipation moved with varying speeds toward realization on the various questions involved.

Everywhere, however, the Jews saw themselves as having achieved or being near to achieving the aim of being recognized as publicly and privately equal German citizens. Riesser's principle of 1830 seemed justified theoretically and practically by its total success. Only Mecklenburg-Schwerin stood apart from the rest of the country. There the emancipation à la Hardenberg that had been accepted in 1812 was rescinded, and there were none of the typical concessions of 1848; indeed, the medieval practice of patronage Jews was revived in 1851. But the spirit of the time is truly reflected in this petition from the Christian magistrate of Güstrow to the ministry:

> The idea of state servitude has disappeared from the national consciousness, and not even the renewed pressure upon the Jews will revive it. . . . It will be impossible to reduce the Jews to the point at which they were held a hundred years ago when they are members of political institutions, and participants in the sciences and arts, producing men who are venerated by the fatherland and whose names will probably forever be linked with the culture of the present epoch. [Dubnow, II, 333.]

The ministry, however, in its wisdom, did not bother with the petition. How the protectorate over the Jews was destroyed in the last of the German lands will be related.

The Mecklenburg resistance should serve as a reminder of the persistence of the voices of hatred in those days of progress and hope. Probably the most influential of this sort of thing was Naudh's (a pseudonym) *The Jews and the German State*. Naudh's views are already racist and, while he advocates baptism, he doubts its effectiveness. Naudh was as muddle-headed as most hatemongers. The following is a typical excerpt of his work:

> They have not even condescended to making their Sabbath fall on Sunday, although the difference is nowhere required by their religion and could be given up without dogmatic contradiction, as it was introduced arbitrarily; an honest existence is impossible, if they also respect the Sunday of the Christian state. [*Op. cit.*, p. 51.]

Richard Wagner's statement of 1850 about the events of 1848 is more representative:

> When we fought for the emancipation of the Jews, we did so for the abstract principle rather than for any concrete case, without any knowledge of this people and with actual repugnance at meeting them. In spite of all the speeches and publications for emancipation of the Jews, we instinctively recoiled from any active contact with them. [Wagner, p. 10.]

X

IN THE SECOND EMPIRE

Emancipation was constitutionally complete with the founding of the Second Empire. The law of the North German Federation in 1869, it became the law of the entire Reich in 1872. Emancipation this time was a result of the movement toward national unification, as in Austria in 1867 it had been a result of state reforms consequent upon military defeat. Switzerland, the last of the predominantly German states to emancipate, was also the last Western state, doing so only in 1874 after having first lifted the restrictions on Jewish freedom of movement in 1866. To that date, Jews had been confined to two communities in the canton of Aargau. Over-all, the Jews themselves and the feelings of the Germans were well prepared for unhindered equality.

Interest in things Jewish continued to diminish among broad strata of Jewish society. The best-known Jewish writers of the period, like Berthold Auerbach, tended more and more to avoid Jewish themes. The future of Judaism received no attention from the most distinguished Jews in the humanities, with the exceptions of Lazarus and the linguist, Wilhelm Steinthal. The ties of religion were coming undone. Piety and charity often substituted for the exercise of cult and faith. Historian Martin Philippson graphically described the results for the religious communities:

> The administrations [of the communities] set a bad example. They looked on their communities as they would on a financial undertaking, like a manufacturing plant or commercial complex whose costs have to be reduced as much as possible. There were few temples, few rabbis, few schools, no furthering of Jewish interests . . . everything had to be cheap, for Judaism was an old institution that was to be abandoned; no "educated" person could feel a warm concern for it. [Elbogen, p. 273.]

Nevertheless, Judaism was preserved both practically and as an object of research. Heinrich Graetz, for example, pursued his *History of the Jews from Ancient Times to the Present* over a period of decades. Running to eleven volumes, the first of which appeared in 1853, this was the first comprehensive, scientific treatment of the theme, although the work was somewhat partisan. Graetz, however, correctly stressed the national character of Jewish history, although this view ran directly counter to prevailing contemporary opinion. Although it was thoroughly rejected by many Jews, this view nonetheless roused the ire of the historian Heinrich von Treitschke and turned him in 1879 against the Jews. Graetz was a teacher at the theological seminary founded in Breslau in 1854. This institution stood ideologically halfway between the Orthodox Rabbinical Seminary and the liberal Higher Institute for the Science of Judaism (founded by Abraham Geiger), both established in Berlin in 1872. Since every rabbi had to have a university degree but could not prepare at the same time for the rabbinate in the university, these institutions were developed as modern replacements for the moribund Orthodox educational system of Central Europe. The Higher Institute for the Science of Judaism was open to everyone, and persons of all shades of opinion taught there, whether or not they were theologians, or Jewish or Christian. Women were admitted. The danger remained, however, as Leopold Zunz, the ancient master of Judaistics who had never held a university chair or gained public recognition, realized, as long as such work as his was excluded from the curricula of German universal education. Zunz lamented that "the slighting of Jewish authors, even of converted ones, will continue to exist in Germany until all the universities have Jewish professors lecturing in Jewish history and Jewish literature." (Kobler, II, 356.) This necessity, unmet before 1933, is only now being acknowledged.

Judaism was not emancipated when the Jews of Germany were. As Germans, however, Jews were making their honest contributions to the country. More than a thousand Jews fought with Prussia during the war of 1866. Six thousand Jewish soldiers fought in the war with France, 448 were killed and 327 received the Iron Cross. Theodor Fontane, the German author of *The German War of 1866*, evaluated the Jewish contribution to the war: "It would seem that they had vowed to destroy the old concept of their antipathy to and incapacity for war." (Fontane, I, 43.) Despite their record, Jews were proscribed from the officers' corps until the First World War. They were permitted in the reserve officers' corps only in Bavaria.

A long line of outstanding Jews played important parts in the preparation for and construction of the empire. Riesser, who died before the founding of the Reich, was one of the first members of the *Deutscher National Verein*. Eduard

Lasker was one of the most important of the group that drew up the constitution and laws of the Reich. Ludwig Bamberger was a cofounder of the Reichsbank and originated its gold standard. Lasker and Bamberger supported Bismarck both in the diet of the North German Federation and in that of the empire until 1878, when no doubt was left about Bismarck's reactionary tendencies. Paul Leband, a Jew, was the author of *Deutsches Staatsricht* ("German Constitutional Law"). Levin Goldschmidt, who had pioneered commercial law as a university specialty, created the German law of commerce. In 1869 he was elected councilor of the Federal High Tribunal for Commerce (*Bundeshandelsbergericht*) and in 1872 was appointed to an ordinary professorship, the first unbaptized person to hold such a post. He was a legal advisor to Emperor William I during the Emperor's arbitrament of a Canadian-United States border controversy. Goldschmidt, who considered himself joined to Judaism by piety only, wrote in a pamphlet published four days after the outbreak of war with France:

> On July 19th, France declared war on Germany. Until the nineteenth there were political parties in Germany: Conservatives, Liberals, Democrats, and Ultramontanes, followers of the military state, and federalists, whatever their names. From July 19th on, there are no longer political parties: there are only sons of the fatherland or traitors. [Kohler, II, 251.]

All these men were non-converted Jews, as was Moritz Ellstadter who was Baden's minister of finance after 1866 and whose system of taxation served as the model for the Prussian system.

It may be of some interest here to sketch the figure of the

convert, Eduard von Simson. Great-grandson of Joachim Moses Friedländer, one of Frederick II's patronage Jews, and great-nephew of David Friedländer, Eduard Simson was born in Königsberg in 1810 and was baptized at the age of twelve. When he was eighteen, he appeared before Goethe with a recommendation from the composer Zelter, Goethe's close friend and later president of the Goethe Society. Like Stahl, Simson's thinking remained at a considerable distance from Judaism. We have seen him earlier in his role in 1848–49 as president of the Frankfurt parliament and leader of the delegation to Frederick William IV. As president of the Reichstag, which post he held until 1879, he offered the imperial crown to William I at Versailles. Simson was named president of the court of appeals in 1869 and, ten years later, president of the Reich Court. Probably no one of Jewish parents, before or since, obtained such dignities in Germany.

We turn now to an analysis of the legal form of the equalization of rights. The constituent assembly of the North German Federation met in March, 1867. There were four Jews among its membership: Bamberger; Lasker, a National Liberal; and Johann Jacoby, a radical progressive who anticipated the German militarism that would come as a consequence of unification. Some 420 Jewish communities sent petitions asking for legal equality, those of Schwerin-Mecklenburg making the deepest impression. With Lasker's support, the petitions were rejected on the grounds that it was the responsibility of the individual *Lander* to decide such issues. The representatives of Mecklenburg protested. Since the desire was to avoid burdening the constitution with a "Jewish article," the following resolution was designed to satisfy the protests. It was taken in November, 1867: "No member of the Federation can be denied the right to stay, settle, or to exercise a profession or own real property in a community for reasons of religion or for not belonging to the given state or community." (Dubnow, II, 338.) Saxony complied, but there was some resistance in Mecklenburg. Because of this Wiggers, the Mecklenburg deputy, petitioned the assembly "to abolish the medieval conditions which are incompatible with the constitutions of the Federation." It was clear from the debate that the epoch of Riesser was waning. Lasker, for example, covering his weakness with an assumed nobility, explained that "as a matter of principle, I never take the floor in matters which are so close to me and my co-religionists, since it might appear that I am speaking selfishly." (Dubnow, II, 339.) Wigger's motion carried, and this statute was signed into law by the king and Bismarck on July 3, 1869:

> All restrictions on civic and constitutional rights proceeding from religion are herewith abolished. In especial, participation in state, municipal, parliamentary, and administrative activity should be without respect to religion. [Dubnow, II, 340.]

Even Mecklenburg now had to conform. Prussia was the first state to meet the requirements of the federal law, which at last restored equality in Bavaria. From 1872 onward, judges, teachers, and university teachers who were Jews were permitted, to a limited extent. Actually, conditions were liberal only for a few years. Unconverted Jews were still excluded from positions in the higher state administration and from universities. Excepting the few Jewish schools, there were seventy-eight Jewish teachers among the total of 64,750 Prussian primary teachers; and there were eighty-nine Jewish judges of a total of 4,400 judges. In institutions of higher learning in 1900, there were sixty-two Jews of a total faculty of 6,247. Although the federal law of 1869 abolished regulation of the private conditions of the Jews, the laws and regulations of the individual states—and this continued until the Weimar Republic—still governed the religious communities. Thus, for example, the rule of 1850 continued in force in Prussia, under which Christian churches received financial help and privileges from the state, but the communities of the synagogues received nothing. Rabbis were not entitled to such special considerations as were accorded to the clergy as a class, and they were not considered indirect employees of the state, unless serving as military chaplains, prison chaplains, or in other state institutions.

The beautiful peace was of short duration, although it was possible for a rabbi to be chosen to deliver the sermon in Nuremberg in 1878 on the occasion of the victory at Sedan. Agrarians, junkers, and other conservative elements were unsympathetic to the Jews. They disliked their capitalism, their influence in the liberal press, their role in the progressive movement and, later, in social democracy—despite the very little attention given Jewish leftists to the Jewish question or to Jewish interests. Indeed, the liberals began to avoid association with the Jewish cause, and no successors arose to replace Lasker and Bamberger. Nonetheless, the liberals did remain relatively more friendly to the Jews, and the Jews continued to cast most of their votes for the liberals. Jews had exerted great influence in this way for decades—especially in municipal politics and especially in the big cities. The socialists, and the Jews among them with particular strength, saw Judaism as archaic, and they rejected it, as they did every religion, although they demanded equal rights for all, including Jews. The Catholic *Zentrum*, on the other hand, was frequently benevolently neutral toward the Jews but remained opposed to liberalism. To the satisfaction of the *Zentrum*, the delegates of the Jews voted against the *Kulturkampf* laws, but liberal Jews favored them. They saw in it the triumph of secularism over the clericalism that they had so long sought to defeat.

The "Founders' Scandal," first revealed in 1873 by Lasker, brought to light the unsound underpinnings of certain financial corporations of the early Reich. Many middle-class people, many Jews among them, were among the victims. But Lasker and the ruined Jews were ignored by agitators, who fastened attention on the participation of Jews in the swindle. The slogans of the "Jews and Golden International" quickly revived, and a certain Otto Glagau asserted that he had precise information to show that nine-tenths of the founders were Jewish:

> Jewry . . . knows nothing but commerce and, of it, only usury and haggling. They do not work themselves but have others work for them. [Elbogen, p. 281.]

There was simultaneously a Catholic press crusade against the Jews as enemies of Christendom and propagators of materialism, in Austria particularly. *The Talmud Jew*, a defamatory pamphlet written by a professor of theology, August Rohling, in 1871, was given away in great numbers throughout Central Europe. In a memorable trial, Rohling was in the end declared a liar and a cheat.

XI

HATRED OF JEWS AS ANTISEMITISM

At Bismarck's adoption of a conservative policy in 1878, the left wing of the National-Liberals, including Bamberger and Lasker, allied itself with Richter's Progressive party under the new title of German Enlightened [*Freisinnige*] party. Although Bismarck's turn was not motivated by a fundamental animosity toward Jews, he did encourage and tolerate the reactionary forces that were gathering strength at this time for the most vicious anti-Jewish campaign since 1819. While the campaign did slowly abate, the movement managed to persist—operating publicly and covertly, and increasingly maliciously—until the 1933 catastrophe. Every idea that contributed to the growth of Nazism was developed. It was impossible to refute objectively—however prudent one might be—the thoroughly inhuman charges against the Jews.

The hatred of Jews had two forms; later in Austria especially there developed absurd combinations of the two. The first presented itself as the Christian position and was based upon the stale accusations that we have frequently met with. The second added nothing to the list of charges but sprang from a new point of reference—race. The logic inherent in this position could not lead to demands for corrective reforms but to expulsion and physical destruction. Its second novelty was the racist postulate that everything connected with the Jewish race and its "malice"—an assertion always taken for granted—everything created by Jews was by necessity bad. Since Christianity was itself "Jewish," it followed that it was "evil." Apart from the misfortune it heaped upon the Jews, racist hatred became increasingly disastrous for Christians, who in ignorance tried to come to terms with it. They failed to see that they were thus laying Christianity open to the same onslaught: a sacrifice of the Christian cultural tradition to scorn, destruction, and hate.

In 1878 Berlin court preacher Adolf Stöcker founded the Christian-Social Workers' party, soon thereafter dropping the word "worker" under some pressure. The development suited the authorities, and Minister von Puttkammer was openly pleased with Stöcker, who was winning over many of the discontented lower-middle class at his sometimes church-held meetings. Stöcker spoke before the Prussian chamber of deputies in 1880:

> For me the Jewish question is not religious or racist. Since full emancipation has already been effected, it is not a constitutional question. It is an ethical-social question, with roots in religion, race, and constitutional law; in its manifestation, however, it is a social-ethical question of great national significance. [Dubnow, III, 9.] Israelites are a foreign people and can never become one with us, unless they are converted to Christianity. [Stöcker, p. 39.]

Wilhelm Marr's pamphlet, *The Victory of Jewry over Germandom*, first appeared in 1871 but was widely distributed only after 1878. Its hatred of Jews was of the "antisemitic" form. In his view, hatred of Jews manifested the struggle of opposed principles and did not arise from religion. His conception of the struggle of principles would underlay the materialist-biologic metaphysics of National Socialism that would itself serve as underpinning for the policy of genocide. Richard Wagner, whose thinking followed the lines of Marr, said in 1881:

> It is an established fact that I consider the Jewish race to be the born enemy of pure mankind and of everything that is noble: it is quite clear that we Germans . . . will perish through them, and I am probably the last German who knew how to maintain himself against an overbearing . . . Judaism. [Reichmann, p. 191.]

In 1881, the writer Eugen Dühring announced his discovery that the Jews were the worst of the Semitic tribes. They had given nothing to the world and had borrowed everything from other peoples. The Jews were unredeemable; a Jewish antisemite could not alter his Jewish nature. The aim of the Jews was exploitation and domination of the world. Dühring rejected the Bible and Christianity, taking his antisemitism to its logical conclusion—a sharp rejection of Christianity:

> For Christianity today to oppose itself to Judaism—if only on moral grounds—would be to attempt to render the harmful harmless through one of its own branches, that is, through a conscious part of itself. The adherents of the Christian tradition cannot turn decisively against Judaism. [Dühring, p. 32.]

Paul de Lagarde wrote just a few years later:

> You have to have the heart and skin of a crocodile not to

> feel for the poor, exploited Germans and . . . not hate the Jews . . . or to squash like vermin those who take up the defense of the Jews or speak on their behalf out of "humanitarian" considerations. We do not negotiate with trichnines or bacilli; we render them harmless swiftly and thoroughly. [Lagarde, p. 339.]

The demands of Nazism echo in the words of the professional Jew-baiter Theodor Fritsch, in 1887: One of his "Ten German Commandments" declared: "You should know that, together with your fellow Germans, regardless of faith or political opinion, you have one common, implacable enemy. He is called Jew." (Fritsch, p. 346.)

Antisemitism was not merely the free, undisturbed distribution of this kind of publication in great numbers. An Antisemitic League was established; and many other organizations voted to expel their Jewish membership; there were International Congresses for Antisemitism, and antisemitic political parties were successful, as in 1893 they gained a total vote of 263,000 and sent sixteen antisemites to the Reichstag. The Conservatives resolved in 1892: "We oppose the Jewish influence upon the life of our people. It is often overbearing and destructive. We demand a Christian authority for Christians, and Christian teachers for Christian schools." The Federation of Farmers was similarly antisemitic. Boycotts of Jewish merchants were often staged under the leadership of the Conservatives, especially around Christmas, often with the effect of financially ruining the Jews of the small villages. Social barriers were raised; "restricted" resorts, hotels, and rooming houses appeared.

Following the visits of traveling agitators in 1881, there were riots with arson and looting in the small cities of Pomerania, Western Prussia, and Brandenburg that continued until it was decided—probably in consequence of the devastating pogroms of Russia and Poland—to call in the police and militia to restore order. There was a ritual murder trial in 1891–92 in Xanten, but the results disappointed the fanatics; even the public prosecutor pleaded for acquittal. When the case was discussed in the Reichstag, Stöcker, a member between 1881 and 1911, declared with his usual kind of duplicity:

> I cannot conceive of the Jewish cult demanding the murder of people or using blood for any imaginable purpose. But the quarrel is hair-splitting. Can anyone deny that history shows the sufferings of Christians, especially children, at the hands of the Jews and the loss of life through Jewish fanaticism and superstition? [Dubnow, III, 43.]

Thus the words of the court preacher.

We turn now to Treitschke, the erudite historian who had declared in two 1879 articles in his *Prussische Jahrbucher* ("Prussian Annuals") his dissociation from the antisemitic movement because of its "dirt" and "brutality" and because he did not want to attack emancipation. He added a good measure of oil to the flames nonetheless. He saw in antisemitism the outbreak of "a deeply-seated and long-smouldering anger," not "hollow and groundless" but revealing the "natural reaction of the Germanic ethnic sentiment against the foreign element." He lamented that Jews refused to become Germans, and he could not abide the prospect of "a thousand years of Germanic sentiment being followed by an age of German-Jewish mixed culture."

> Even in the most educated circles, among men who reject religious intolerance or nationalistic pride, there echoes the cry: "The Jews are our misfortune." A Jewish

> demand for the recognition of Jewish nationality will upend the legal bases on which emancipation rests. There is only one way to fulfil such a wish: Emigration, the foundation of a Jewish state. . . . There is no room on German soil for a double nationality. [A Word about Jewry.]

Thus, overheated nationalism, unsated by the founding of the Reich, was rather encouraged by it to turn against and exclude non-conforming groups. It would do the Jews little good to be good Germans, if they remained Jews at the same time. A totalitarian mentality was widespread long before the idea of a totalitarian state was hatched. The Jews, thinking themselves "good Germans," and humanitarian and liberal non-Jews were surprised by this kind of attack, and their response as a result was relatively weak. This state of affairs would be improved gradually but insufficiently, in part through the continuing progress of assimilation and in part through a growing Jewish self-awareness. But at that time the sudden storm that swept over the Jews caused extreme despair. It is the subject of many of the letters of Berthold Auerbach in the year 1880:

> This is why we have worked so hard and so long—to obtain this barbarity in an educated German [Treitschke, of course]. To have lived and worked in vain! This is my overwhelming impression. . . . I am desperate at the arrogance and distaste shown for Jews in even the most liberal people, awaiting only the proper moment to come to light. [Kobler, I, 270 f.]

Popper-Lynkeus, an Austrian Jew and social philosopher and physicist, wrote six years later:

> Basically, antisemites are simply hostile to certain people. They are united by sheer hatred; . . . an anarchic

> grouping who are trying to channel their desires into a system. . . . Wherever men call themselves antisemites, all Jews . . . must immediately feel solidarity. . . . This is sad but necessary. [Popper-Lynkeus, pp. 129, 132.]

The most radical attack mounted by the antisemites before the time of the Weimar Republic was the petition organized by school principal Bernhard Förster and Max Liebermann von Sonneberg. Nearly a year in preparation, it was submitted to Bismarck in April, 1881, with the signatures of 267,000 persons, including 4,000 students. Bismarck received it in silence. The petition called for the restriction of immigration, exclusion from all responsible state administrative positions and from the posts of judges sitting singly; it asked that Christians alone be allowed to teach in the primary grades and that Jewish admission to higher schools and universities be made exceptional; a special census of Jews was requested. The letter that had accompanied the petition claimed that Bismarck and the government agreed with this expression of the people's will. The petition ran:

> For some time the minds of serious and patriotic men of all walks of life and of every party persuasion have been worried over the excessive growth of the Jewish ethnic element. The expected complete blending of the Semitic and the Germanic elements, a hope formerly cherished by many, has turned out to be a chimera, despite the complete equality before the law. We are no longer faced with a situation of equality but . . . with the increasing predominance of Judaism, whose influence springs from racial peculiarities which the German nation neither can nor will accept without losing its own soul. . . . Based . . . on laws created under Jewish influence . . . the Jewish race has been able to exercise its malevolent influence, not only on

> the economic conditions and thus the wealth of the German people, but seriously poses a threat to German culture and religion. These dangers will, as a matter of course, increase insofar as Jews succeed in penetrating in hordes into the professions and, especially, the civil-service posts heretofore closed to them. [Dubnow, III, 18.]

There was sharp opposition to the position from more rational elements, and it became the subject of an interpellation in the Prussian diet in November, 1880, at the request of the Enlightened party. Speaking for the government, Count Stolberg declared that it had no intention of circumventing the basic law of equality. On the other hand, August Reichensperger, a Conservative, lauded the antisemites and asked government assurance that it would not alter its administrative practices with respect to the Jews. The great physician, Rudolf Virchow, of the Enlightened party, asserted that the government's complicity with the antisemites made it responsible for their actions. The leader of the Enlightened group said eloquently:

> I know very well that the Chancellor has his head and his hands full with this matter. In order to bring things to focus . . . we submitted our petition, for we want to see the suppression of the reactionary party that is bringing shame upon our country. . . . Beware of arousing the wild passions in the undisciplined masses of the people. Do not arouse the beast in man; it will stop at nothing. [Dubnow, III, 21.]

XII

GERMANY AND WORLD JEWRY

Apart from the influence of the medieval Moors, no people has had such a lasting impact on the Jews as the Germans of the era between the last third of the eighteenth century and 1933. Germany both gave and received much in respect to the Jews. Jews borrowed much in turn from Germans. In the process, however, the central values of Judaism were largely unrepresented until the last two decades of the period. By then it was too late. "The thousand-year-long history of the Jews in Germany has ended," Leo Baeck announced in 1933.

The sources of German influence on the Jews were several. Among the chief ones were German literary culture, particularly of the classical epoch; German ideas and values as spread by the Jews of Germany and Austria; the trends in Jewish thinking from the time of Mendelssohn, which were deeply marked by their openness to German ideas and owe their very existence to a German-Jewish cultural blend. There were also political influences from Germany and Austria and, finally, the countervailing force of antisemitism, which nullified most of what had been created by Germans and Jews within the German cultural sphere and willingly, often enthusiastically, accepted by Jews in other countries.

We shall examine cultural influences first. It should be borne in mind in this regard that during the two-hundred and fifty years preceding emancipation the bulk of Western Jews, except the small numbers in Italy and Holland, were largely untouched by their environment. Jews came to participate in the ideas and achievements of Western culture through the agency both of the eighteenth-century German spirit that insisted on humanism and idealism and the activities of Mendelssohn and his followers. In those countries where the Jews strove for emancipation—with the exception of the eastern provinces of Austria—cultural involvement proceeded by way of assimilation, that is along the lines established by Napoleon, Joseph II, and Hardenberg. This was an assimilation chiefly to the German spirit and German nationality. Assimilation was only a partial factor in the east, where the situation was much more a matter of people learning equally from one another.

The German sphere of influence was extended by means of German-Jewish assimilation (including religious reform) to the Jews of Hungary, Scandinavia, Holland, England, and North America, and to a lesser extent to the Jews of France and Italy. Up to the end of the nineteenth century, a considerable number of rabbis came from the countries of Central Europe. They were naturally influenced by Germany and German Judaism, and their effect on the Jews of many other countries can hardly be over-estimated. As early as the eighteenth century, Jews in Eastern Europe had begun to take an interest in Germany. This was at first an individual matter, as, for example, the instances of the anonymous Polish Jew whose poetry was reviewed by Goethe, or Salomon Maimon, the outstanding philosopher from Lithuania who learned to read German long before he spoke it and who died in 1880 in the castle of his patron Count Kalckreuth in Silesia. In the Polish regions of the Austrian empire, it is difficult to distinguish between German cultural influences and the political effects of Germanization. About one hundred German-Jewish elementary schools were founded in Galicia after 1787 by Mendelssohn's disciple, Herz Homberg. They had to be abandoned, however, in 1806 without having brought about the assimilation for which they aimed. Nonetheless, the upper strata of Galician Jews voluntarily assimilated only a few decades later; the young became enthusiasts of German lyrics and philosophy, made Hebrew imitations of German poems, and translated the German classics, especially Schiller, into Hebrew. Galicians came to study in Germany, as did, for example, Salomon Rubin at Göttingen who wrote his doctoral thesis on Spinoza and Maimonides. In this Galician German-influenced Jewry lie the origins of Martin Buber.

Russian-Jewish students began to appear in Germany in substantial numbers around 1850. Schelling and Alexander von Humboldt were among their sponsors. And Germany had its attraction for those who could not travel to her: the Russian-Jewish enlightenment—the revolt against old-fashioned Orthodoxy—was based upon German literature and in particular on Schiller, who was taken as the theme of the young Martin Buber's bar mitzvah speech. The extent of Schiller's influence even before 1850 is reflected in the *Memoirs* of Pauline Wengeroff:

> Schiller's poetry came like a breath of spring into the oppressive and stale atmosphere of the ghetto. When Jewish youth began to read foreign works, they took up Schiller first; he excited them and formed their knowledge of Ger-

> man. Soon, knowledge of Schiller's works was part and parcel of an educated Jew's program of studies; he studied the Talmud and Schiller, and the latter by the very same method as the former. Every important sentence was studied separately and meditated aloud; questions and possible answers followed each other . . . until a satisfactory solution was found . . . as well as the meaning . . . which was supposed to be hidden *behind* the words. . . . The reason for such popularity is to be found in the essence of Schiller's poetry . . . in his idealism, which considered everything from an ethical point of view. [Wengeroff, II, 34 f.]

There are many testimonials of Schiller's influence in the first part of the nineteenth century. Thus:

> The scholar in talmudic casuistry carries Schiller's *Don Carlos* with him, and he oscillates between the free thought of the Marquis Posa, which he extols, and the needle-sharp distinctions of his masters [in the talmudic school]. [Jellinek, p. 21.]

In Austria, unlike Russia despite all the sympathy there for Germans, Germanization was sometimes the achievement of a single generation. Karl Emil Franzos of Czernowitz typifies this process. As a student in Vienna and Graz, he was a member of the Teutonia fraternity and took part in the fraternity's Rallies in Berlin in 1868, signed the resolution to the German universities at the beginning of the Franco-German War, spoke at meetings of German nationalists, belonged to the committee to prepare the victory celebration, and was fined in 1870 as one of the leaders of a German Nationalist student beer party. His approach became less reckless only after the experiences of 1880, by which time he was writing the tales that literary historian Ludwig Geiger (son of Abraham Geiger) sardonically described as "the cries for help of a good German who laments the decline of German culture . . . which had formerly tried to penetrate the east." (Geiger, p. 261.)

One of the most productive roads to German thinking and feeling for the Jews of Eastern Europe was Yiddish, which, with German, was the world language of the Jews of the nineteenth and into the twentieth century. The writer and storyteller M. I. Bin Gorion spoke as late as 1918 about this experience of the Jews of the Ukraine:

> A foreign language became our own. . . . We no longer knew that we were living in a foreign country. . . . For us children in school, Hebrew and Yiddish were like the two eyes that see as one.—Thus, I shall never forget the horror I felt . . . when I heard the Talmud translated into Russian for a disciple from the Caucasus who did not understand Yiddish. . . . And when my heart yearned for the spirit of the people, I was driven to Germany, to the motherland of my language, so to speak. [Bin Gorion, p. 51.]

Language was not the least of the reasons behind the fact that many Russian Jews did not flee in time before the Germans during the Second World War after warnings from the Soviet authorities. Buoyed up by favorable memories of German attitudes during World War I, the Jews simply did not believe that the Russians would for once have told them the truth. Hundreds of thousands paid for this mistake with their lives.

Official Russian policy toward the Jews was influenced around 1800 by the early reform proposals of Austria and Prussia. Derschawin, a member of the Russian senate preparing a memorandum on the subject, received two proposals from emancipated Russian Jews asking for permission for instruction in the German language. In the statute of 1804 Jews were permitted to found schools of their own which could adopt German. Later, German examples were important in the reform of Jewish schools and education in Russia in general, and it was in this connection that the Russian government invited Max Lilienthal, a Munich Jew, in 1841. His mission, however, came to nought after several years.

Austria continued its policies of Germanization in the non-German-speaking regions for as long as possible. In 1857, despite the slow pace of assimilation among the widest circles of the population, Galician Jews had to declare themselves either German- or Polish-speaking, since Yiddish was not recognized. Until the last quarter of the century, the Jewish upper strata declared itself to be German-speaking. Later, as a consequence of antisemitism, they declared themselves Polish-speaking. In Bohemia and Moravia in 1900, some 54 and 23 per cent, respectively, declared themselves Czech-speaking. The situation was difficult for the Jews in these countries; during the Prague riots they were attacked as Germans; in Eger they were attacked as Czechs. In Hungary, despite energetic Magyarization, a quarter of the Jews declared themselves German in 1900.

Germany also played a role internationally on the Jewish question. Bismarck did so when he, along with the Western Powers, called for the equality of the Jews in Rumania during the Berlin Conference of 1878. Ten years earlier, he had similarly intervened at the behest of the Alliance Israélite Universelle. Rumanian obligations to the Jews, however, were largely paper promises. Karl Anton von Hohenzollern-Sigmaringen could, therefore, cynically tell his son, Karol of Rumania:

> The Jewish paragraph obtruded on us by the Congress is

> nothing but abstract humanitarian words. These conditions are to be regulated by legislation alone, and I am convinced that at a later date, with the exception of the Alliance Israélite, nobody will give a damn how these decrees are carried out. [Kobler, II, 424.]

German antisemitism played a pernicious role internationally. It would be no exaggeration to argue that it, not the Jews, deprived Germany of its role as a world power: Up to the explosion of antisemitism and well into the First World War, the Jews in general were more closely attached to Germany than to any other country. In France antisemitism became strong but lost importance after 1900. The most harmful effect was upon Russia. Marr's pamphlet had been immediately translated there. The harsh Provisional Order of 1882—by which Jews lost nine-tenths of their areas of permitted settlement in Russia—was officially justified in part by a reference to the burgeoning antisemitic movement in Germany. The Austrian Chargé d'Affaires Trauttenberg reported to his Minister of Foreign Affairs in Vienna in 1881:

> This renewal of the Jewish question, which had hardly quieted down, will cause many difficulties for the government. In view of the sympathies here for the antisemitic movement that is spreading through a great part of Germany, the English moves designed to forward the equality of the Jews can hardly have the desired success. [Kobler, II, 440.]

These moves were not successful, and the pogroms continued. The fact was not regretted by the antisemites of Germany; Popper-Lynkeus noted that "Stöcker publicly stated that . . . he would not have stopped his agitations against the Jews, even if he had foreknowledge of how the

Jews were to be treated in Russia." (Popper-Lynkeus, p. 146.)

The full harvest of antisemitism is described in a 1909 lecture by Professor Ehrlich of Czernowitz:

> I myself still belong to a generation which saw no other solution to the Jewish question than a complete dissolution of the Jews in Germandom. This . . . also applies to the Jews here in the East who are settled among Slavic peoples. We always regarded the Jewry of the East as an extension of the German position of power deep into the territories of foreign people and empires. If this whole plan has to be abandoned now, it is due to the antisemitism which has taken hold of the German people. . . . German politics can be carried out by Jews only *with* Germans and never *against* Germans. . . . Whoever cares for the interests of the German people in Austria and the world position of Germany . . . can only regret . . . that this rather stupid student caper, antisemitism, has played such an important part that it has robbed the Germans of a position of power or at least of a field of influence which used to reach from the Bohemian Forest to Odessa. . . . A people with some sense of politics would have known how to secure these advantages. The future historian who will write the history of Austria's ceasing to be a German state and the bulwark of German culture in the East will have to give over a rather long paragraph to antisemitism. [Trietsch, p. 18 f.]

XIII

ASSIMILATION AND ZIONISM

A certain Theodore Fritsch declared in 1887: "All Germans have now recognized the reasons for antisemitism, and educated youth has enthusiastically taken up the banners of Germandom against the cunning enemy." (Fritsch, p. 1 f.) Today we know that such fantastic assertions cannot be argued out of existence; phenomena of this kind must be carefully studied and the state must take such measures as befit a civil community faced with a social crime, as, for example, it must do with regard to pornography. In those days people reacted only to the outward signs of the hatred against the Jews. The causes went untouched. Both Jews, and Germans who were free of antisemitism, were without answers—let alone the right answers—to provocations. The Jews asked themselves: What can we do? Are we not Germans? Are we not German enough? While it was true on the one hand that intermarriages were increasing (with the children as a rule lost to Judaism) as were conversions, this could not be a solution for German-Jews who wanted to remain Jews for reasons of self-respect or faith. They found themselves in that dual position that both Treitschke and his German opponent and Jewish defender, Theodor Mommsen, rejected out of hand. The philologist Hermann Steinthal pointed to the flaw in this attitude (which was honestly held) in a statement around 1890:

> No—there is no conflict between being a Jew, a German, or merely a human being: the three interpenetrate in such a way that we can be one only if we are also the other two. The Jewish German can be among the best of Germans and the German Jew, one of the best of Jews. . . . Therefore we love our German fatherland and are grateful to it; today we can be good Jews only if we are good Germans, and good Germans only if we are good Jews. The phrase "the chosen people" is for us an historical memory of special religious-ethical significance, an admonition . . . to self-examination and humility; it means that we Germans come from non-German forbears but find in the blending of Jewish-German nationality a greater reason for humanitarian and ethical action. Together with the prophets, it is Lessing and Herder, Kant, Fichte, and Schiller, Goethe and the two Humboldts who arouse our enthusiasm—and they could not have emerged from any other people, just as the prophets could not have arisen outside of Israel. [Steinthal]

Four years before Steinthal's statement, a number of Jewish students in Breslau expressed themselves even more sharply in their "Words to Our Co-religionists":

> No one can any longer doubt that . . . the whole life of the people is poisoned as a result of the fanatic teachings [of antisemitism], that . . . we Jews are scorned by wide strata of the population, hated, or at best considered as foreigners, and not as equal citizens; but it is painful to see these feelings manifested in the circles of the best

educated. . . . We . . . who are still in the midst of the academic life, feel the abyss that lies between us and those we still call our fellow-students. This . . . poses a danger on a wider scale, if the consequences of this attitude are taken into account.

The authors called for the establishment of an "association of Jewish students," which was soon set up:

Such an association will, by its very existence, rekindle the consciousness that we are Jews, which has nearly disappeared, and that we are part of a great unity of historic and cultural significance. . . . We can anticipate . . . the objections [to this]: "You should not set yourselves off, should not stress your differences, but rather should try to obliterate them and assimilate yourselves." Well, this method has had a good trial. . . . But efforts along these lines . . . have not produced the desired effect. . . . We represent the principle—and we will embody it in our behavior—that, simultaneously, we can be Jews and Germans in the best sense of the word. We strive to be men who fulfill faithfully and enthusiastically every demand the state makes of its citizens, and we desire to work with our Christian co-citizens in the solution of the great tasks of our times. [Weil]

Here was the view of themselves that Jews would maintain as a self-respecting basis for assimilation until the bitter end when its foundation was destroyed. Many of these students participated in the founding of the Central Association of German Citizens of Jewish Faith, organized by German Jews after the ritual murder trial at Xanten and the unbridled, mordant incitements against Jews by the antisemite Hermann Ahlwardt. Raphael Loewenthal prepared the program of the

Central Association. In the pamphlet entitled *Patronage Jews or Citizens?* Loewenthal wrote:

> We are not German Jews but German citizens of the Jewish faith. We are anchored in the ground of our German nationality. We have no more in common with Jews of other countries than have German Catholics or Protestants with Catholics and Protestants of other countries.

The Central Association looked on antisemitism as a "curable illness" and set as its major goals education and legal protection. Its successes were, in fact, in opposing unlawful actions taken by the civilian and military authorities against Jews. It also took a sharp line in 1896 against political Zionism, which was then beginning to make its appearance, and held that German Jews were linked to each other by religion and history but not by a Jewish nationality: "Birth, education, language, and sentiment have made Germans of us, and no trend of the times can estrange us from our dearly beloved fatherland."

The onset of Theodore Herzl did not shake this approach, but it was not the first time that it had been questioned from the Jewish side. But no one—even outside of Austria and Germany—had ever presented the Jewish national demands so effectively or armed them with such up-to-date techniques of Realpolitik. Herzl himself acted without knowledge of his predecessors, including the most important of them, Moses Hess, who had proclaimed in 1862:

> Jewry is above all a nationality; its history goes back several thousand years and marches hand-in-hand with the history of mankind. . . . So long as the Jew denies his nationality, because he does not have the character to confess his solidarity with an unhappy, persecuted, and scorned

people, his position is bound to become more and more insupportable with every day that passes. [Hess, pp. 17, 40.]

Among Jews of public standing, only the historian Graetz acknowledged Hess. But he had been hailed by another early Zionist:

> From your newest work . . . I saw with pleasure that you are advocating the renewal of our people. . . . Such work . . . is the more worthy because it is not long since everybody deprived us of our nationality. [Kobler, II, 389.]

The generally hostile Jewish view toward such undertakings is apparent in these words of Abraham Geiger:

> Jerusalem is an honored memory of the past . . . it is not a hope for the future, not the place where a new life is to develop. . . . Honor Jerusalem as you would the great dead, but do not disturb its peace. [Elbogen, p. 299.]

Beyond charitable endeavors (which gradually increased from benefactions of minor proportions to something considerable) German Jews wanted nothing to do with the kind of solidarity that Hess preached. Indicative of the general view are these words by Auerbach in 1872 on the occasion of a plan for the emigration of Rumanian Jews to the United States:

> I consider the plan very dangerous. What happens if there is another major persecution of Jews in Galicia or elsewhere? Will another congress then effect another emigration? . . . If the Jew has a justified cosmopolitan trait, he also has a patriotic one. This concept of mass emigration would add something of the gypsy to the position of the Jews. [Kobler, II, 421.]

Political Zionism was born in 1882. That was the year that saw the formation of the Khoreve Zion in the wake of pogroms in Russia, the emigration of idealistic pioneers to Palestine, the establishment in Vienna of the first nationalist Jewish student association (the Kadimah) by Nathan Birnbaum of Galicia, and the anonymous publication in Berlin of Leo Pinsker's pamphlet, *Auto-Emancipation.*

> Civil and political equality is not enough to give the Jews respect among nations. The right means, the only means . . . is the auto-emancipation of the Jews, their equality as a nation among nations by the acquisition of a home of their own. [Pinsker, p. 29.]

Pinsker's views were completely rejected almost everywhere in Germany, although they were enthusiastically received in Eastern Europe:

> To expect the Jews to give everything up, now that they have adapted completely to the national life of the people, would be silly fantasy. What is wrong with the man is his Russian-nihilistic viewpoint. [Kobler, II, 45.]

Herzl, as a young man, had been quite removed from such questions. He was born in Budapest in 1860 of a family originally from Turkey. He was educated in the German assimilationist manner, came to Vienna in 1878, where he joined the fraternity of Albia and became one of the most zealous partisans of German nationalism. But critical of the antisemitism of his fraternity, he gave up active membership in 1883; he had not yet developed specifically Jewish interests. As a successful playwright, he covered the famous Dreyfus trial in Paris for the Viennese *Neue Freie Presse.* This experience determined his mission in history. *Die Judenstaat*

("The Jewish State") was written in 1895 and published in 1896. In it Herzl demanded of the Great Powers that they concede to the Jewish people sufficient territory "to create a home assured by public law for those who do not want to be, or cannot be, assimilated."

His motivation is revealed in various parts of his book:

> The antisemitism of the present must not be confused with the hatred of the Jews in former times, although in certain countries hatred of Jews is inspired by religion. Today the main current of the anti-Jewish movement is different. In the chief antisemitic countries it is a consequence of emancipation. By the time the educated people saw the barbarity of the exceptional laws and freed us, it was too late. Law could no longer emancipate us in our home countries. Oddly, we had developed into a middle-class people in the ghetto and emerged as formidable competition for the middle classes. . . .
>
> It might be thought an obstacle for us that we no longer have a common language. We cannot use Hebrew as a language of communication. . . . Yet the thing is quite simple: Each one retains the language which is the beloved home of his thoughts. . . . We shall remain over there what we have been here all along, just as we shall never cease to love with sadness the home countries from which we have been expelled. [Herzl, pp. 25, 75.]

Herzl was not only a writer and an excellent speaker. He was a man of action and an accomplished diplomatist. In the eight years preceding his untimely death in 1904, he successfully fostered the cause of political Zionism, despite great difficulties, setbacks, mistakes, and controversy, and he became a decisive factor in the fate of the Jews. His largest following was inevitably in Russia and Rumania where the

Jewish situation was intolerably bad; in Germany only students for the most part were on his side at first. Chief Rabbi Güdemann of Vienna opposed him. When Herzl was planning the first Zionist congress for Munich in 1897, he was condemned by the president of the German society of rabbis:

> The efforts of the so-called Zionists to found a Jewish state in Palestine are opposed to the messianic promises of Judaism as contained in Holy Writ and later religious sources. Judaism obliges its faithful to serve the fatherland with every devotion and to further its national interests with all their heart and all their forces. . . . Religion and the love of fatherland, therefore, oblige us to ask all those . . . who have Jewish welfare at heart . . . to abstain from the congress that is still being planned despite all warnings. [Dubnow, II, 342.]

As a consequence, the congress was held in Basel, where it was attended by two hundred delegates and three hundred guests and correspondents. Its official language was German, as it was to be in all later congresses; speeches in Hebrew were translated into German. Defining Zionism as the return to Judaism that precedes the return to the homeland, Herzl was elected president of the organization's Action Committee with its seat to be in Vienna. In 1898 he met three times (in Constantinople, in Mikweh Israel, and finally in a solemn audience in Jerusalem) with Emperor William II, asking for the Emperor's intercession with the Turkish sultan in favor of Zionist aims.

XIV

GERMANY AND AUSTRIA BEFORE THE FIRST WORLD WAR

Although the meetings between Herzl and the German emperor produced no results of a practical kind despite the emperor's evident sympathy, they were of great symbolic significance. Twice, Jews had approached the leading German monarch during the period of the Age of Emancipation. Fifty years before, Riesser had come as a member of the Frankfurt Kaiser delegation, symbolizing in his person the symbiosis of emancipation and the assimilation of the German Jew. Now, Herzl, as the founder and leader of the Zionist organization symbolized the failure of emancipation, the impossibility of assimilation, and the campaign to bring about a German-Jewish alliance. Neither view of the future would long be accepted. The assimilationist coexistence was smashed, and the alliance did not materialize. That both possibilities offered historical chances and that Germany met neither is a measure of the tragic relationship between the two groups; its consequences for both cannot even yet be fully determined.

After this glance at the general perspective, we turn to the Jewish situation in Germany before the First World War. Rising antisemitism, most strongly in evidence in the decade

1878–88, continued unchecked but became less visible. Opposition forces among both Germans and Jews gained strength, but there were foreboding signs in the activities that went on beneath the surface. Indeed, certain obvious evidence remained clear enough. Literary prominence was bestowed upon the *Foundations of the Nineteenth Century* by Houston Stewart Chamberlain, an Englishman turned German who became Richard Wagner's son-in-law. The work portrays the history of culture as the struggle of virtuous Aryans and vicious Semites. In order for the German spirit to triumph, the Jews must be expelled. Shortly after the appearance of the book, the spirit, so-called, suffered a defeat in the last German ritual murder trial in Konitz in 1900. The riots which broke out were quelled by troops. Antisemitic witnesses at the trial were accused and convicted of perjury; the editor of an antisemitic newspaper was jailed for his slander against tribunal personnel. There were nine antisemitic deputies to the Reichstag in 1903, six in 1908, 22 in 1911, and thirteen in 1912. These received a total vote in 1912 of 461,000; in 1913 the total was 376,000.

The days of militant antisemitism seemed numbered. But Minister of Justice Schönstedt's reply to a 1901 interpellation is revealing of the time:

> I do not deny the excellent qualities of Jewish notaries, their honesty, conscientiousness, and sense of duty, but I cannot overlook the fact that a great part of the Christian population mistrusts the Jew, whereas the office of notary presupposes special trust. The same must be said of the appointment of Jews as judges. [Dubnow, III, 459.]

An investigation into the activity of the tireless Jew-baiter, Fritsch, to determine whether he had blasphemed and offended the Jews was suspended in 1913 by the district court of Leipzig on the grounds that the blasphemed was the pre-Prophetic God from whom the idea of ethical universal monotheism had developed and which only a few religiously and spiritually immature Jews still worshipped. Moreover, Fritsch's attacks, it was held, were only against "those few individuals" who still adhered to the Talmud and who were thus outside the Jewish religious community. (Feuchtwanger, p. 5.) This decision put Jewish Orthodoxy and the God of the Patriarchs and of the Covenant of Sinai outside the protection of the law of the state.

If the Jews had had more peace during this period, it might well have served to divest the Jewish question of its thorns. In the decades up to the first war, conversions—averaging 115 a year in Prussia in 1840—rose to 204 per year. Just before the war, more than 30 per cent of the marriages of Jews involved a non-Jewish partner; the figure had been 17 per cent at the beginning of the century. While the absolute number of Jews in the population rose 112,000 in the period 1871–1910 (when the total was 615,000), the proportion had fallen from 1.25 per cent to 0.95 per cent. In economic terms, the wealth of Jews had now reached its high point but had not caused any considerable conflict. In all cultural fields, Jewish progress was remarkable; and assimilation remained the basis still for all creative work. By 1912 religious orthodoxy had made a partial recovery, succeeding in the establishment of the anti-Zionist world group, Agudas Jisroel.

The liberal wing of the religion, nevertheless, continued to be much the strongest; it sought unconditional assimilation, going so far as to oppose immigration of Jews from the East as a danger to assimilation, to the fight against antisemitism, and to the modernization of religion. In public statements, the label "inferior" was applied to Russian Jews and state assistance was asked to combat them. In politics, liberal circles inveighed against the Zionists, whom Ludwig Geiger depicted as enemies of the fatherland and unworthy of civil rights. He pleaded for the exclusion as dangerous foreigners of Russian Jews from German communities. His kind of extremist view was rare, however. The Centralverein, in dissociating itself again from Zionism in 1913, averred:

> We want no international solution to the question of the German Jews. As Germans on the soil of the German fatherland, we desire to be part of the culture of Germany and to remain true to our religion and our sacred community. We decidedly welcome German Zionism insofar as it is intent on securing a home for the dispossessed Jews of Eastern Europe or on heightening the Jew's pride in his history and religion. But we sharply distinguish between our views and that kind of zionism which denies German national feeling, sees itself as a guest within a foreign host people, and conceives of itself as a Jewish nationality. [Congress of March 30, 1913.]

One result of this statement was the resignation of many Zionists from the Centralverein; it had been more surprising that they had belonged to it at all. The Anti-Zionist Committee was formed in 1913; it dissociated itself from Zionists, whom it publicly considered "bad patriots, agitators, and disturbers of the peace."

Martin Phillipson's *"New" History of the Jewish People* (my stress, au.) shows how far the disorientation in thinking had gone. Phillipson called the concept of the Jews as a people "an old lie." Zionists themselves were unsure and confused on this point. They often held a double position within the nation and found themselves in conflicts of loyalty from which they could not extricate themselves because they also gave complete loyalty to the cause of assimilation. Thus, in 1914, the famous economist Franz Oppenheimer:

> I do not strive for assimilation, but I am assimilated. I am a German, and I am as proud of this as I am of my Jewish antecedents. I am happy to have been born and educated in the country of Kant and Goethe, to speak their language, and to have absorbed their culture, art, science, and philosophy. To be a German is as sacred to me as my Jewish heritage. . . . I combine within myself the Jewish and the German national consciousness. I and my friends stand firmly on the Basel program, and our good German sentiments do not hinder us from being good Zionists.

Upon the premature death of Herzl, the Zionists were led until the war by David Wolffsohn, a Cologne merchant, and after 1911 by Professor Otto Warburg. Then the German Zionists split into "radicals" and "revisionists." The radicals opposed assimilation; the revisionists looked to a reconstruction of the national culture in Palestine but did not seek it in the diaspora or—least of all—in Germany.

While German Jews of the nineteenth century felt no sense of solidarity with the Jews of the East and—with the exception of Baron Moritz Hirsch—little aided them by charity, the situation changed as a consequence of the work of Paul Nathan. While traveling in the Near East, he studied the situation of the Jews and in 1899 inquired whether the foreign office might give diplomatic protection to a Jewish assistance organization and its schools. The project was deemed useful; in 1901 the *Hilsverein* . . . , the "Assistance Society of German Jews" was founded. Himself a liberal and assimilated, Nathan created a network of Hebrew schools in Palestine and a benevolent society that was the largest yet organized. It assisted some 700,000 Jewish emigrants, chiefly from Russia and Rumania, between 1905 and the outbreak of war. The greatest number of the emigrants went to the United States; some 210,000 of the emigrants received complete financial subsidization from the society.

During the period under consideration in this section, the western provinces of Austria stood under the sign of hatred of the Jews. The phenomenon, introduced from outside about 1880, appeared both as antisemitism and in its Christian aspect, the latter as well as the former giving rise to considerable excesses. The two trends were often in strange alliance. The Jewish situation improved only in the last few years preceding the war, an amelioration arising—unlike the situation in Germany—from the relative sympathy of government and administration toward the Jews. There were three political groups propagandizing the hatred against the Jews. They were: the Christian-Socials, who fought "the Jewish-liberal persecution of Catholics"; the German-Nationalists, who harangued against the "unjustified encroachment of Jews on public affairs"; and the Antisemites, who fought the alleged exploitation of the middle class. This juncture of disparate elements—the German-Nationalists were politically radical and anticlerical—was described by the cleric and Jew-baiter A. Kannengiesser in *Jews and Catholics in Austria-Hungary* (1896):

> Ludwig Pfenner, Ritter von Schönerer, Prince Liechtenstein, Professor Scheicher, Doctor Lueger, Pastor Deckert —all were agreed in the common notion of antisemitism . . . although each had different starting premises. The lower middle class, the professionals, the factory workers, the lower-echelon civil servants, the nobility, and the clergy —all the masses tiring of the yoke of liberalism—at first

> had a merely vague feeling, which later grew into overpowering conviction, that their true enemy was the Jew. Hence, it was quite easy to bring them under a single banner bearing the single, highly charged word: Antisemitism. . . . Consciously or unconsciously, the antisemites became the valuable tools of religious renewal. . . . The clergy unfurled the banner of antisemitism in the newspapers, at popular meetings, at voting rallies, even from the pulpit. [Kannengiesser, pp. 149, 154, 157.]

In this manner the older form of the hatred of the Jew was preserved, or rather renewed. And this explains the meagerness of Christian opposition to race hatred in Austria up to the time of the Nazis, when racism was turned upon them.

We will look a little more closely at the Christian-Socials. As a party, it was organized by Dr. Karl Lueger and Father Ludwig Pfenner out of the Society for the Protection of Trade. Lueger asserted that he had the support of clergy and people. Actually, he had most success with the Pan-Germans of Ritter von Schönerer, with whom he collaborated. Lueger's aim was the abolition or reduction of Jewish rights. Inciting the lower middle class and the students to street rioting, he obtained majorities in the Viennese community council—he was allied with the Antisemites—in 1895 and 1896. After a long resistance on the part of the emperor and the government, he was confirmed as mayor of Vienna and held that office for ten years. Jews were expelled from all municipal posts and were harassed in their civil and economic lives. The high point of Lueger's power was reached in 1907, when his party sent thirty-three deputies to parliament. After his death in 1911, the Christian-Socials seated only three deputies. Lueger, the public speaker, shall be represented here by a few passages from an 1896 speech:

> Everywhere the Jews are sovereign, and the Christians are ruled. Like the farmer, the professional too has become the slave . . . of international Jewry. . . . I know only one destructive element in Austria and that is the Jewish liberal party; it is the dragon . . . that has shackled the Germans and keeps them prisoner. I am proud that I have wounded the dragon severely; I shall see to it that these wounds remain open. The dragon must be slain in order that our dearly beloved German people can be freed from its captivity. [Kannengiesser, pp. xv ff.]

While the Christian-Socials subscribed to hatred of the Jews from the start, Schönerer turned decisively against the Jews only in 1885. In 1880, for example, he had among his collaborators on the Pan-Germanic Linz Program the writer, Karl Emil Franzos, the politician, Victor Adler, and the historian, Heinrich Friedjung—all of them Jews. Jews were accepted as co-fighters in his "hot battle against the Slavs" at least as late as 1883.

XV

THE JEWS DURING THE FIRST WORLD WAR

After 1918 a favorite accusation of Jew-baiters was Jewish responsibility for the war and Jewish responsibility for German defeat. For many years and at least until July 25, 1914, Albert Ballin, a Jewish friend of the Kaiser, worked to avoid the war with England. When war began in August, 1914, Rathenau devised the plan—immediately accepted—for acquisition of the raw materials that formed the basis of the German war economy. In his memoirs the last chancellor of the empire Prince Max von Baden recalled Rathenau's great despair over the collapsing of the front in the autumn of 1918 and his talk of ways to salvage the situation. "A cry from the depths of the heart of a great patriot," was Von Baden's description of Rathenau's guidelines for mass conscription, published in the *Vossische Zeitung* (October 7, 1918). Von Baden also relates that the "Jew Warburg" (Max Warburg, the banker), during the negotiations preceding surrender, implored the high command to keep fighting. When his efforts failed—we may recall that it was Ludendorff, the fiery Jew-hater, who lost his head in the crisis—he addressed a conference in the Chancellor's office in these words:

> To me it seems strange that I, a civilian, should exhort the military today by exclaiming: Keep on fighting! I know that my only son, now in training, will be in the trenches within four weeks, but I entreat you not to make an end now. [Prince Max von Baden, pp. 344 and 380 ff.]

This, in general, was the extent of Jewish guilt for the war and of the Jewish "knife in the back." These examples have been of civilians. Were there deserters at the front? General Von Deimling adjudged the Jewish military contribution in these terms:

> We must not forget that thousands of Jews went to the war voluntarily—that thousands died heroes' deaths for the fatherland—and that thousands were crippled for life. In my corps the Jews fought as bravely as their Christian comrades, and to many of them I presented the Iron Cross.

The youngest of all volunteers was the thirteen-year-old Jew, Joseph Zippes, who lost both legs; among the oldest was Reichstag deputy Ludwig Frank, a Social Democrat who died at the front in 1914. In all about 100,000 Jews were under arms, and some 12,000 were killed. Detailed research after the war was unable to provide the exact figures on the participation of Jewish soldiers from the separated territories to the east and west, but there were 84,000 from the rest of the empire, in absolute terms a very high percentage of the 555,000 Jews of German nationality in the empire as a whole. Of those studied, 78 per cent served at the fronts, more than 10,000 were volunteers, some 30,000 received decorations, more than 19,000 were promoted, and over 2,000 became officers. Of the 1,100 members of the Jewish Fraternity-Convention of Students, 991 were under arms. Among the approximately 10,000 fliers, there were 120 Jews, a percentage higher than that of Jews in the general population. One of them, Wilhelm Frankl, who was killed in action, was a holder of the order *Pour le Mérite*.

The mood and hopes of Jews in the services are revealed in many letters. Deputy Frank, mentioned earlier, wrote:

> I am doing frontline duty like everybody else. . . . But I do not know if French bullets have been advised of my parliamentary immunity. I have the greatest desire to live through the war in order to help construct the inner foundations of the Reich. At the moment, however, my place is at the front in the line with the others, marching cheerfully like them and expecting victory. [Kriegsbriefe, II, 20 ff.]

A reserve lieutenant, Fritz Meyer, who was killed in the war wrote:

> I am happy to be able to testify in bloody earnest for the truth of our idea; the flame of our love for the German people is alive within us stronger than ever. That the dishonest voices of calumny have, unfortunately, not yet been silenced at home certainly does not discourage us. . . . What more do they want than our blood? Let them continue their study of racism with the blood shed by our co-religionists. Enemy bullets do not bother with such distinctions. [*Kriegsbriefe*, II, 54.]

A Sergeant Henle, also killed, wrote in a letter:

> Just as I am well aware of the great honor of fighting for my dear fatherland at the front and of sharing in the victory, I want also to have a voice later, when it will be used to stand up and fight for the equality of our co-religionists in every field. [*Kriegsbriefe*, I, 158 f.]

But what specifically was the attitude of Zionists to their homeland? A soldier, Leo Cahn, wrote from the front:

> At dusk we lit the candles . . . in a circle of our non-Jewish comrades, who looked at the Channukah lights with great reverence. . . . The war will have shown that we national Jews are good Germans too. [*Kriegsbriefe*, I, 149.]

The final example is from a letter by Reserve Lieutenant Alfred Kraus, who died in the war:

> For you . . . and some of your fraternity brothers, the war will be a salvation: I see on the horizon a new race of men like Bar Kochba. Wonderful that forty-five of our fraternity brothers have been drafted. . . . See that you finish the recruit training. In 1813 they were ready much quicker! The Zionist girls should learn nursing. . . . The Zionists of Austria and the Lodges should build a reserve hospital! I hope we soon shall paddle all our enemies—one after the other. Gentlemen of the Triple Entente, this spirit should keep your ears pinned back. To a happy reunion, here or there! [*Kriegsbriefe*, I, 42 ff.]

Thus, it was not only liberal and Orthodox Jews who declared for Germany in the war; it was not only the Centralverein that exhorted that "Jews should do more than merely their duty for the fatherland": Zionists did so, too, interpreting their program in this way:

> A German Zionist who takes up arms against Germany's enemies acts not only in fulfilment of a civic duty but out of the consciousness . . . of, at the same time, defending like every other German his specifically German personality. [Feuchtwanger, p. 65.]

So German, then, so in conformity with the aims of Gabriel Riesser were those who, often more intellectually than feelingly, professed themselves to be national Jews. It should be no great wonder, therefore, that one of the most popular German war songs—the Austrian Rider's Song: "Over the forest's rim hover two blackbirds"—was by a Jew, Hugo Zuckermann. He was killed early in the war.

The assimilationists, pleased by the Zionist professions of love for the fatherland, saw in this a confutation of the concept of Jewish nationality they opposed. Ludwig Geiger went as far as to proclaim a permanent end of relations between German Jews and Jews of countries at war with Germany. In 1916 in his book *Germany and Judaism*, the famous philosopher Hermann Cohen, who had called on world Jewry before the war to show reverence and gratitude to Germany, wrote:

> Thus, in these times of epoch-making fatefulness for our people, we, as Jews, are proud to be Germans. For we are conscious of our task to convince all our co-religionists the world over of the religious significance of Germandom, of its influence, of its rightful claim over the Jews of every nationality, in religious development as in general culture. We consider ourselves, as German Jews, participants in a central cultural power that is called upon to unite peoples in the sense of a messianic humanity. Thus, we reject the view that it is our historic role to undermine peoples and tribes. Whenever there reappears an earnest desire for international understanding and for truly-founded peace among the peoples, our example will stand as a model proving German hegemony over all the foundations of the life of the soul and the mind. [*Ibid.*, p. 39.]

Cohen is quoted in some detail because he bears witness not to the mindless accommodation of a mediocre man but to the religious conscience of an eminent Jew; despite all the contrary forces, this was the degree of the German-Jewish symbiosis in the first part of the twentieth century. German Jews saw Germany as having a right to religious authority over all of Jewry; the final product of this symbiosis was the Nazi decision to destroy the Jews.

The Jews of France and England—in the sense of an assumption of civic duties and as a result of the assimilation that had ensued upon their own emancipation—naturally opposed Germany; would a Christian of those countries have been permitted to do otherwise? Simultaneously, sympathy for Germany among the Jews of Russia, the neutral countries, and—at first—the United States was far-reaching. The cost of this was high in Russia, where Jews suffered mass deportations into the interior of the country, were victimized by pogroms in Lemberg and other conquered cities, and endured horrors that were only to be eclipsed by Hitler's mass murders. We find in the records of the Evangelical Hospital of the Misericordia in Koenigsberg in 1916 this entry:

> While there was still no priest and the hospital (in Suorelki) was filled, the pious rabbi of the place took care of the wounded and dying. Since he knew only the Old Testament, he had the "Our Father" written down for him, learned it, and read it to the Sisters to see if he pronounced it correctly. Then he prayed with it over the suffering and dying after speaking his own words of comfort, in order to give them the company of their own holy prayers. [Bloch, p. 603.]

In the United States, Jews from the eastern countries in particular were sympathetic to Germany; after the United States entered the war, their Yiddish newspapers were subjected to censorship because of friendliness to Germany. The Yiddish-American poet Morris Rosenfeld wrote in one of his pro-German poems:

I am a stranger to the Teuton.
It is the Jew in me who speaks.
But bless the German flag
Where it flutters over Russian towers.

My song is for the German nation.
Long live the Kaiser and his land.
Three cheers for his courage and his flag.
Three cheers for his blessed hand.

In an editorial of September 11, 1914, concerned with the mostly anti-German press in the United States, the *Berliner Zeitung* commented:

> In view of this mass hysteria against us, it is indeed heartening to see the manly fight of the German-American press. . . . The Jewish press assists it . . . quite energetically. In general, it is indeed a pleasure to see how the Jewish element . . . decisively takes the part of Germany and manifests an active will to help everywhere.

Within the framework of the present survey, we cannot treat even cursorily the highly interesting Jewish policy of the Central Powers in the occupied East and within the international community during the war. On the other hand, we have to report briefly on how the Jews fared in Germany during the war. Early in the war, the government suppressed anti-Jewish currents and subjected antisemitic newspapers to censorship. Those Russian Jews who were domiciled in Germany could request acceptance into the army. Civil peace was fairly well maintained until about 1916, when the situation worsened and attacks on Jews increased. A pamphlet by a certain Fritz Siebert asserted:

> We should be able to tell the Jews openly and truthfully that we always shall harbor the suspicion that a

> foreign way of thinking permeates their trading- and middle-mannish spirit and that in their advice they do not attend sufficiently to the characteristics of the German people. . . . We shall not hinder Jews who want to be assimilated. Jews . . . who want to remain Jews should take the consequences and should be listed in Germany as second-class citizens or as foreigners. [Siebert, p. 31.]

The tone here was still mild; it was shortly followed in quite a different mood.

On the instigation of an antisemitic deputy in the Reichstag, a Dr. Werner, and a certain military authority, the Prussian Minister of War carried out a census of Jews in 1916. Although the methods of the census were attacked by Jews and despite the fact that Jews were purposely sent behind the lines for the census, it still appeared that the percentage of Jews at the front was relatively higher than that of Christians. Nonetheless, accusations against Jews increased; in particular they were accused of profiteering by holding back supplies of food. (The authorities, however, engaged in this kind of agitation only during the last year of the war.) In a hate-pamphlet published in Berlin in 1918, the Jews were accused of causing the war. It contained a poem which ended: "We see their grinning faces everywhere, except in the trenches." Jewish organizations again failed to take effective action in the face of such calumnies. However, during the war they had done much to assist Jews from the occupied countries of the East, shipped into Germany by the army to work in war industries, and to help the 450,000 Jews from Bucovina and Galicia who were resettled in Austria. For the history of the following decades, these first personal contacts with non-assimilated Jews of the East turned out to be crucial.

XVI

IN THE WEIMAR REPUBLIC

One Nazi writer dubbed the Weimar Republic "a Jewish paradise." What was the actuality of this Eden? A Jew, Hugo Preuss, was a leading architect of the democratic constitution of the republic. During the deliberations in the national parliament over the inclusion of a clause on minorities in the constitution, recognition of the Jews as a national minority was rejected, insofar as it concerned an individual national life. Unlike other countries, Germany was not obliged by the terms of the peace to protect its Jewish minority, as this appeared unnecessary under the prevailing legal situation. Jews were now being appointed to civil-service positions that had earlier been denied them and occupied a goodly number of important posts. Politically and constitutionally, the Jews achieved full emancipation under the republic. At the same time, from the fall of the empire to the period of inflation and later—and not just after the inflation—the Jewish economic and social situation substantially worsened.

It is a cheap truism that a number of Jews or descendants of Jews—none of whom, with the exception of the socialist writer, Gustav Landauer, had anything in common with

Judaism, religiously, nationally, or spiritually—were radical left revolutionaries. Such were Rosa Luxemburg, Kurt Eisner (murdered by the half-Jew, Count Arco), the pacifist Leviné, and the poets Erich Mühsam and Ernst Toller. The overwhelming majority of Jews, however, were liberals of the middle- to upper-middle class who rejected revolution, and there were conservatives also. While there may have been individual Jews among those profiting by the inflation, the genuine culprits were non-Jews, the industrialist Hugo Stinnes; President of the Reichsbank Rudolf Havenstein; and the financial adviser to Chancellor Cuno, Karl Helfferich. The middle classes, including the Jews, bore the brunt of the losses. And while there was an abnormally large number of Jews among professionals, these never played much of a role in the heavy industry that was so crucial to political development, or in the cartels of trade or industry. None of the leading members of the bitterly criticized Young Plan or of the Dawes Commission was a Jew.

To be sure, Germany was confused by a lost war, a revolution, and inflation—facts borne with equal pain and patience by the Jews in the population. There is not the slightest particle of truth to the suggestion that the new state was a "Jewish republic" or its parliament a "tool of Judaism." Had this been true, the Jews would have been able to defend themselves against the new flood of hate, a flood that surpassed that of the 1880's. Actually, the Jews were lamentably helpless and were unable to move the state to outlaw even the most obscene of the pamphlets, with their incitements to violence and killing.

A certain Walter Liek proclaimed in 1919:

> The true seat of sickness in the national body of Germany is the influence of the Jews. . . . The emergence of

> Judaism in leading positions allows us to recognize . . . the actual state of the disease.

Liek asserted that there would have been no revolution without the Jews, despite certain abuses (of which the Jews, he said, were certainly not without guilt either). During the war, William II had been "politically ruled by the German Department of the Pan-Judaic state." Its aim was alleged to have been the prevention of victory, not the destruction of Germany. The Jewish Central government in London, however, was said to have forced a peace of "unconditional surrender." (Liek, p. 15.) In *The Innocence of Those Beyond*, an anonymous book of 1921, we find:

> Emil Rathenau . . . who, among all the Jewish "friends," was the closest to the Kaiser and even had a special direct telephone line to him, remodeled his house at Victoria Street 3 a few years before his death, and decorated it with a bas-relief of sixty-six bowls displaying the heads of decapitated kings. At his death his son, Walter, replaced him; although he did not have the Kaiser's attention to the same extent as his father, his fateful advice was also willingly accepted. [*Ibid.*, p. 126.]

These are merely two examples of a literature of flood proportions. It included among others the notorious *Protocols of the Elders of Zion* that was distributed in enormous editions for many years. Fabricated in Russia in 1905, the *Protocols* are essentially a plagiarism of an 1864 pamphlet attacking Napoleon III. This had been in the form of a dialogue in Hell between Machiavelli and Montesquieu. In the *Protocols* Machiavelli's words are put into the mouth of the representative of Judaism, and the whole is presented as excerpts from the minutes of the first Zionist congress of

1897, according to a speech of the "exilarch" Herzl. This fiction was brought to Germany through the translations of the notorious Fritsch and Ludendorff's collaborator, Gottfried zur Beek. The German antisemites were undeterred by the London *Times*' having unmasked this fraud in three articles in 1921. They countered that its content, "right or wrong," was clearly consonant with the Jewish spirit. The *Protocols* held that "three hundred wise men of Zion" controlled the fate of the world. Rathenau was considered to be one of the "wise men" by his murderers, by the members of the German-National Schutz and Trutz (one of many antisemitic associations), by the Federation of Frontline Soldiers (the Steel-helmet), The Young-German Order, and the University Ring of German Ways—all of which were founded after the war. As one of the wise men, Rathenau was believed to have wanted to destroy Germany and establish Jewish world rule.

The novels of Artur Dinter are a noisome mixture of pornography and pseudo-theosophy. In 1920 in his *The Sin against the Blood*, he wrote:

> We should recognize . . . that it is in a very specific race of men that the spirits who renounced God . . . like to take shape for the purpose of diverting an unsuspecting mankind from its true and divine destiny through the temptations of selfishness and wild sensuality. . . . Then we should never cease fighting and wrestling until this devilish race be made harmless for mankind. Not until they shall be rid of this unsavory race will the German people be able to fulfill the destiny marked out for them by God—to lead all people . . . toward spiritual intensification and a deepening of the mind. [*Ibid.*, p. 273.]

The innumerable fictions of this miserable kind had their influence upon the people. There were other sorts for the more sophisticated tastes of the "educated" classes. Such is Wilhelm Stapel's *Antisemitism* (1920), in which Heine's "Lorelei" is analyzed:

> Whereas Eichendorff's rhymes are somewhat soft and refined, the rhymes of Heine are sharp, pointed, and rather hoarse. . . . As one relaxes in the innervation of the words: "Ich weiss nicht, was soll es bedeuten," the words immediately attack us, grip our arms, and force us to lift our shoulders, with outstretched palms—a typical Jewish gesture.

One could qute from hundreds of such authors, books, and pamphlets, without even touching on the storehouse of the antisemitic newspapers and magazines of those years. More drastic in effect than the books, which had at least to be read, were the verses of the following sort that spread among the people:

> Crack the Jew pack on their heads
> And win the future.
> Our colors will snap proudly in the wind
> When Jewish blood streams down our sabers.

The salvationist aspect of secular antisemitism, not yet understood by Jews or Christians, grew more and more plain. It was a demonic, irrational hatred of Jews, with a clear method, as the Nazi regime would rapidly demonstrate after its "victory" over the so-called "Jew Republic." Yet among the quotations given so far there is not a single one from a Nazi source. For the Nazi arsenal generated nothing new; it was a collection and a skilful use of evil that had long since been prepared. When it is realized how far emancipation was reversed in this period, it is remarkable that there were but few physical attacks upon Jews. But there were occasional outbursts, chiefly in Upper Silesia and Berlin. In the latter city these occurred for the most part during the Kapp coup. Although accused of being in bondage to the Jews, the government did nothing to quench the flames of hatred.

It is estimated that there were some 100,000 East European Jews in Germany after the war. For the most part these people had been sent from Poland and Lithuania by the army for war work; some of them were refugees of pogroms in the Ukraine and Poland. These poor folk were under constant attack. Unfortunately, a representative of the Association of German National Jews publicly opposed them and spoke of the "danger from the Eastern Jews." Bavaria ordered them expelled within five days in an order of May, 1920. The Prussian situation was similar: raids were organized in Berlin, and the captives were shifted to the prisoner-of-war camp Wünsdorf near Zossen. On the appeal of the Workmen's Social Assistance Society of the Jewish Organizations of Germany, the authorities investigated the situation; in 1923, however, hundreds of families were expelled from Germany.

Academic youth threw caution to the winds and joined in the antisemitic movement. The Student Fraternity, after the so-called Eisenach Decisions of 1920, refused on general principles to accept Jews or descendants of Jews. Mixed marriages were penalized with expulsion. The High Kösener Union, another fraternity, followed suit the next year. It formulated the following definition: "A person of mixed descent shall be a Jew, if one of his four grandparents was a Jew or if it appears otherwise that he is of Jewish descent." (Scheuer, p. 57.) Antisemitic resolutions strove to outdo one another: in 1923 the Cartellverband of Catholic, Color-bearing German Student Unions was impelled to state: "One reason for the denial of entrance to the Cartellverband shall be semitic descent going back to the grandparents." (Scheuer, p. 58.)

Meanwhile, the supposedly powerful Jews stood by, powerless in the face of this poisoning of their everyday lives. Despite these portentous indications, the Jews were unable to reconcile their differences or raise a consistent defense of their vital interests. They remained split into parties and groups at odds with each other. As before, the Centralverein—which had 70,000 members in 1925—was the strongest organization and spoke for about 300,000 Jews. At the time there were approximately 570,000 Jews in Germany, constituting 0.9 per cent of the total population. Despite the obstacles, assimilation seemed to be increasing still. Of each 100 Jewish marriages in 1927, some 64 were mixed marriages.

During the deliberations over a constitution in Austria, the antisemites unsuccessfully proposed a separate curia for the Jews. The Social Democratic leader and the secretary of foreign relations, Victor Adler (he had been close to the Pan-German Schönerer in his youth), was of Jewish origin. He made *anschluss* with Germany part of the basic law, but its enforcement was prohibited by the Entente. For the rest, Adler cared little for Jewish affairs, like other Jewish socialists in Austria and Germany. It can hardly be surprising, therefore, to find the Social Democratic press of Austria apparently inimical to the Jews. The assimilationists prevented the recognition of the Jews as a nation, an aim put forward by the Zionist National Council, formed after the war. The results of the election for the presidency of the Jewish community of Vienna show the distribution of forces: Assimilationists held twenty seats; Zionists, 13 seats; and Orthodox, 3 seats. For the census of 1923, the German-Nationals succeeded in having a "race" category introduced, but this was filled with such grotesque replies as to make the results useless.

Many refugees from the separated provinces had been left behind after the war. Their return to their homes was sometimes impeded by the continuation of fighting there or by violent pogroms against the Jews. Still, German-Nationals and Social Democrats urged speedy repatriation. In May, 1919, antisemites in the national assembly proposed concentration camps for the Jews. Secretary of State Matthias Eldersch, in pointing out that speedy repatriation was impossible because of the refusal to issue transit visas by several states and for other reasons, said:

> I want to reject the putting of Jews in concentration camps, as proposed by Deputy Kunschak. I would consider this a *Kulturschande*; quite apart from this, such measures would be considered *barbaric abroad*. [Keppel, p. 256.]

There were many deportations later, and Austria rivaled Germany in agitations against the Jews.

XVII

BEFORE THE CATASTROPHE

It is not true, though still claimed, that Germany and its Jews were surprised in 1933 by the institutionalization of antisemitism by the Nazi state. There was no need to have read *Mein Kampf* or other Nazi works to have known what was being prepared under the tolerant and passive approach of the feeble republic. As early as March, 1930, the NSDAP had proposed in parliament a bill for the protection of the German Nation. Its Articles 4 and 5 read:

> Whoever undertakes to deliver German ethnic and cultural treasures to the influence of a foreign race is to be punished by imprisonment for cultural treason. Whoever contributes to the debasement and disintegration of the German race by mixing with members of the Jewish blood community or with colored races is guilty of racial treason.

The proposal hardly dovetailed with the remarks Hitler made to the American newsman Wiegand. Hitler had said "I am not for a restriction of the rights of the Jews." To Wiegand's question about his inclusion of antisemitism in his program, Hitler answered: "The people would not understand, if I did otherwise." (*New York American*, January 5, 1930.)

But this people was taught that all of Germany, from left to right, was under Jewish influence. There was Marx on the left; Lasker, Preuss, and Rathenau in the center; and Stahl on the right, the Nazis pointed out. As the first Reich constitution was said to have been poisoned by Lasker and Bamberger, the Weimar constitution was said to have been contaminated by Preuss. Yet during the nineteen governments of the republic up to 1933, there were only two Jewish Reich ministers of a total of 387 (Preuss and Rathenau), and three men of Jewish descent (Landsberg, Gradnauer, and Hilferding). Among about five hundred civil servants of the Reich from the rank of chief councilor up to secretary of state, there were fifteen Jews and descendants of Jews. At the same levels in Prussia the count was ten Jews among a total of three hundred, with no Jews among the twelve presidents of provinces, the thirty-five presidents of sub-provinces, and the four hundred district presidents. Despite this, word was spread about that Germany was ruled by the secret Jewish government. Other charges against the Jews included racial slurs, Jewish power in "world finance," Jewish wealth, the disintegrating spirit of the Jews and Jewish lack of culture, the "secret laws" of the Talmud, the moral double standard of the Jewish religion, Marxism, Bolshevism, and Socialism—identified with Jewry—Jewish hatred of Christians, Jewish unproductivity, Jewish "disdain" of agriculture and the crafts, and the alleged Jewish domination of trade and the press. Counterarguments and explanations were no longer listened to. On the verge of being outlawed, Jews could be reviled with impunity; published libels were no longer confiscated.

Goebbels' *Angriff* editorialized in the issue of January 21, 1929:

The Jew has immunized himself against all injurious attacks: scoundrel, parasite, deceiver, profiteer—this goes down like water off the back of a duck. Call him a Jew and you will be astonished to see how this hits him, how he shrivels up in front of you: "I have been found out!" . . . We National Socialists know his ways to the smallest detail and we have the courage . . . to take radical consequences. These are: we cannot fight the Jews positively. He is negative and this negation has to be eradicated from the German picture. . . . We cannot discuss the Jewish question with the Jews. One cannot convince someone that one's right and duty is to render him harmless. One must not concede the Jews the same means of defense which would be conceded to any honest adversary. . . . The Jew has no voice in German questions. He is a foreigner, a stranger in our midst who enjoys rights only as a guest, but these he abuses without exception. The so-called religious morality of Jews is not a morality at all, but a guide to deception. Therefore, it is not entitled to the protection and care of the state. The Jew is not cleverer than we, but wilier and more cunning. His system cannot be broken economically . . . but only politically. A Jew cannot offend a German. Jewish calumnies are only honorable scars for a German adversary of the Jews. Whoever is not persecuted by the Jew, or is even praised by him, is useless and harmful. . . . Whoever spares the Jew, commits a sin against his own people. One can be only a servant of the Jews or their enemy. Enmity to Jews is a matter of personal hygiene.

And the "Jewish Republic" put up with all this! The implications of the Angriff make it easy to credit Fritz Marburg's statement in his *Antisemitism in the German Republic* (1931):

[Justice] looks with an antisemitic eye upon the trials

> in which Jews are plaintiffs in cases of forgeries, libels, moral and material injustices. The punishments . . . for defamation against Jews, for offenses against the Jewish faith, desecration of Jewish cemeteries are . . . surprisingly mild. Thus, the Reichs' Court gave a not-guilty verdict in the case of the executive editor of the *Westdeutscher Beobachter* who had written in an article of March 13, 1929, that Jews, following the precepts of the Talmud, used Christian blood in their rites. [*Ibid.*, p. 59.]

There is proof of the desecration of some 128 cemeteries and 50 synagogues in the period between 1923 and September, 1932. Physical attacks on Jews increased in the final years of the republic. Eight Jews were killed in Berlin early in 1930; eight months later seventy-eight Jews were seriously injured. On May 2, 1931, students occupied the entrances to the University of Berlin and attacked all Jewish-appearing male and female students. Many were hospitalized. The attacks continued for hours, and despite the pleas of a delegation of the Jewish students, the university rector took no action and refused to call in the police.

Marburg described the Reichswehr, which had eight Jewish members in 1931, in these terms:

> When on March 1, 1931, a platoon of Reichswehr marched from the parliament on the occasion of celebrations in memory of the war dead, they were preceded by young Nazi marchers with swastikas and steel helmets and accompanied by police. One immediately sensed a kind of symbolic tripartite union of the Reichswehr, the police, and National Socialism. [*Ibid.*, p. 59.]

At a time when the slogan "Germany, awake—Judah, perish!" was very popular, boycotts of the Jews were frequent, as is reflected in these lines:

Buy from the Jew—that is not right.
The Jew never lacks for anything,
Yet the merchants of your country
Skirt the rim of catastrophe.

In Marburg's judgment:

> The economic boycott is felt by the Jew in the worst way. Unemployment among the intelligentsia is increasing, the Jewish merchants are being impoverished and dissolve their businesses, the trader risks his life when he goes out to the villages for customers. On every side, attacks are leveled against Jewish industrialists, bankers, merchants, intellectuals and manual workers which cut off their sources of income and will finally make them destitute. [*Ibid.*, p. 56.]

As a consequence of the general economic slump and the boycott, some 30,000 of the 175,000 Jewish salaried employees were out of work in the period before Hitler; some 40,000 of the 170,000 Jews in Berlin were on the relief rolls of Jewish welfare organizations.

As early as 1919, the nationalist parties refused Jews membership. And with the exceptions of the *Zentrum*, the Democrats, and the left, all parties in one degree or another were inimical to Jews. A German-National, Hugenberg, obviously no "slave" of the Jews, controlled more than half of Germany's newspapers—over twice the combined holdings of the Jewish firms Mosse and Ullstein—after 1919. In Marburg's view:

> The most powerful boost was in the area of the Nazi press, which in 1927 . . . hardly comprised seven publications but which today [1931] includes ten dailies and fifteen weeklies. According . . . to an incomplete listing, in

> 1927 there were 718 German publications that were furthering antisemitism. Support . . . of this antisemitic propaganda has come from quite different circles: from Bavarian industrialists, like Maffei, Hornschuh, Aust, Prince Ludwig Wilhelm, and Baron Cramer-Klett; from tycoons like Borsig, Bechstein, Kirdorf, Siemens, Krupp, Thyssen, Mannesmann, and others. . . . The education of the people in the spirit of hatred of the Jews is completed by the theater, films, and the radio. In big cities as in provincial towns, reactionary plays with antisemitic tendencies are presented on the stage. . . . The most dangerous medium of antisemitic propaganda, however, is broadcasting: many lecturers seize the occasion to weave acid remarks about the Jews into their lectures. [*Ibid.*, p. 57.]

In the light of this relatively unhindered antisemitic development, it is unreasonable to suppose that the rise of the Nazi party took place without there being a parallel awareness of its general program fairly reeking with hatred of the Jews. Whatever may have determined the increasing attractiveness of National Socialism, hatred for Jews doubtless must be given a prominent position. The Nazi party had 64,000 members in 1920; in 1931 there were 600,000 card-carrying members. Nazis won some 1,900,000 votes (not to count the one-third million votes given to Kunze's German Social Party, which was really no less antisemitic) in the 1924 elections, nearly four times the voting total of the open antisemites of 1911. And when there could no longer be any doubt about the aims of the Nazis, the NSDAP won 6,400,000 votes in the fall, 1930, elections. Thereafter their membership grew by leaps and bounds.

Long before its official abolition, emancipation had been drained of value. Despite everything, however, a great many Jews clung to assimilation, although Zionism was gaining followers, especially among the young, who were shunned by their non-Jewish peers. The assimilationists' adherence to the notion of the German essence and their identification with the old ideals—sometimes desperate, sometimes emotionally moving—had often a degree of tragi-comic exaggeration. Constantin Brunner, the philosopher, still averred in 1931 in the manner of Riesser:

> Separatism on the part of citizens of Jewish faith and descent can only be a political separatism for the purpose of struggling on the soil of the people to which the Jewish citizens belong. But it cannot have anything to do with a Jewish nationhood—openly or secretly. Germans of Jewish descent must carry out their struggle for emancipation as Germans. [Brunner, p. 17.]

In Austria, with some differences things ran much as they did in Germany. A characteristic appraisal is found in a letter from Graz to the *Deutsche Hochschulzeitung* in 1923:

> National Socialism has carried its victorious progress to us too and has found a firm foothold in our universities. Many color-bearing students, . . . dissatisfied with nationalist activities without a party tie, have joined the movement, undoubtedly attracted by its sharp accent on racial purity and on the *easily understandable* aims of the national struggle. [Scheuer, p. 62.]

There was one development in Austria that seldom occurred in Germany. The Catholic clergy, though it rejected the racist viewpoint, could hardly be distinguished in its views from the Nazi propagandists. As late as January 21, 1933, Bishop Gföllner of Linz wrote in a pastoral letter:

> It is unquestionable that many Jews have turned from God and are exercising a bad influence in almost every field of our modern cultural life. . . . Degenerate Jewry, in alliance with world free-masonry, is the principal carrier of

> mammon-inspired capitalism. . . . It is not only our right to battle against this pernicious influence; it is, moreover, the conscientious duty of every true Christian. It is desirable that neither Aryan nor Christian should imitate or further, either openly or secretly, these dangers and damages. Formerly, . . . the Jewish population was given places of their own, a ghetto so-called, in order to banish the Jewish spirit and Jewish influence. In the modern world Jews need not be expelled from the country, but a strong dam should be erected by legislation and by the administration to hold back the spiritual excrement and flood of unethicality which threatens to overrun the world, mostly from the side of Jewry. [Czermak-Karbach, pp. 137 ff.]

The Bishop added immediately (it sounds very weak indeed): "But we admit unreservedly that there are noble characters to be found also in Jewry." (*Ibid.*)

"Noble characters in Jewry" . . . with this afterthought many, many a gravedigger of emancipation in Germany, the gravediggers of the remarkable Germany-Jewish symbiosis, turned his back on the Jews and left them to their fate or did worse. In similar fashion the NSDAP *Schleswig-Holsteinische Tageszeitung* on February 21, 1930, concluded:

> The Jewish people as such is poison for the Germans; it is foreign in its essence. . . . The existence of some honest Jews is no argument against antisemitism, just as the existence of many dishonest Jews is no argument for antisemitism.

In other words, insofar as Jews were concerned, actual people were no longer to be regarded. "Nobility" and "honesty" were without meaning; the Jewish people as such were "poison," to be counteracted and eradicated. This was the end of the Age of Jewish Emancipation in Germany.

EPILOGUE

It would be dangerously false to assert the impossibility of Jewish emancipation in the West or in Germany on the grounds of the catastrophe of 1933. But the basic conception of an emancipation granted to individuals but not to coherent groups is suspect, and it is misconceived. A personal assimilation that involves the relinquishment of all or nearly every group characteristic must have been, as it was, torn by impatience (described early in this study), by the failure in German lands to achieve an unconditional realization of legal equality (in fact, historically, legality was steadily restricted), and by that distillation into secular race hatred of religious animosity feeding upon the indescribable misery of the millions of Jews who had not been emancipated from the Tsarist empire and Rumania. The question is not whether the Jews before Mendelssohn were a people or were only a religious grouping. The fact is that the Jews did become a nation by the processes and as a result of the deficiencies of emancipation. This despite half or more of all German Jews disavowing until the bitter end that they were members of a Jewish nation. The idea seemed extraneous and artificial to them. If men have the right to choose the group to which they belong, it was their right to have thought so.

Historically, however, this was irrelevant to the birth and growth of that secular Jewish nation in which membership is given without regard to faith. The development of this national consciousness may come to a point where Jews who feel themselves Jewish by nationality will refuse to be assimilated and will deny assimilation as a possibility for other Jews. They would have no right to do this. While their implicit view may or may not be desirable, reality confutes it. There are always Jews who assimilate and who disappear into another people. Assimilation occurred during and before the Age of Emancipation. Without judging the propriety of assimilation, we must recognize it as a fact. But the fundamental insight of the experience of the emancipation remains valid. Many Jews—not only in Central Europe—realized through the crisis in emancipation that they had been presented with irreconcilable demands. They did not deny the need for emancipation, for the assurance of human rights to Jews whether in a Jewish state or in the diaspora; but they advance it as a claim for a whole community. This is the lesson that the Jews learned. As German history happened, the generations between Mendelssohn and Herzl could not see this. They were sacrificed to the conflict between their Judaism and German education.

The Jews—and not only German Jews, but Jews the world over—loved Germany. It would take much to lessen or kill this love. In *The Jewish State*, Herzl wrote:

> Perhaps we could have disappeared without a trace within all the peoples who surrounded us, if we had been left in peace for merely two generations. But we shall never be left in peace. After short respites, enmity against us again arises. Our well-being seems to contain elements of excitement, for the world has been accustomed by centuries to see in us the most scorned of the poor. Ignorance and shortsightedness fail to see that our well-being weakens us as Jews and obliterates our characteristics. Only pressure makes us cleave again to the old stock; only the hatred surrounding us makes strangers out of us. [Herzl, p. 26.]

These could not have been the words of a Russian Jew: they draw upon the inspiration of the sadness and despair of the assimilated Jew who sees the likelihood of assimilation's failure. There were other possible reactions to this impending failure besides Herzl's. Jacob Wassermann outlined one in his expressively titled, *My War As German and Jew:*

> It is vain to attempt to pull the fangs of poison. They are preparing new ones. It is vain to live for them and die for them. They say: He is a Jew. I am a German, and I am a Jew, one as deeply and as earnestly as the other. They cannot be separated from each other. [*Ibid.*, pp. 122 f., 126.]

Neither the nationalist Herzl nor the assimilationist Wasserman reached the religious depth of Martin Buber, who grew up in the old Jewish traditions in the city of Lemberg yet drew close to Germany as a young man. His was a Zionist outlook, but it was not that of Herzl. He defined his position toward Germany in 1916 and at the same time disengaged himself from assimilationism:

> Those [Jews who consider themselves at home in Germany] assure the Germans that they are not *different* in order not to be treated as *aliens*. But we are different and, yet, in very truth and plainly stated, we are not foreign. . . . This reality we see is familiar, different but not essentially strange, and we love it: the language which taught us to think; the landscape which taught us to see; the creative depth of a great nationhood which has given us this lovely and fateful present. We do not link arms with them but we greet them . . . : Friends, we are underway for both our sakes—and for the sake of salvation. [Buber, p. 25.]

This perhaps expresses the best of the German-Jewish symbiosis—a Judaism that does not deny itself, does not surrender its dignity or pride; strong on its own foundation and open to the world; attached to Germanhood and nourished by its own spirit, it attempts to subordinate both to a higher community: to mankind—by which I mean not a vaguely cosmopolitan idea but a salvific community.

It is not my intention (nor is it possible) to list the achievements of the Jews who accomplished this symbiosis. I decline to submit to the Germans another apologetic catalogue that must always begin with the seven Jews and four half-Jews among the forty-four German Nobelists of 1933 (not to mention the three Jewish medalists from Austria). Such a listing might be valuable in another connection, but not here. Nor is it appropriate to list other great contributions to German culture by children of assimilation (e.g., Heine, Freud, even Marx). They typify only their own situations in their own worlds; they are not examples of the fulfillment of the German-Jewish symbiosis. For that it is essential that it arise from the depths of both the German and the Jewish spirit. Such a kind of blending demanded a tradition, and it would be unfair to expect to find it therefore in the men of the first four generations of the Age of Emancipation when the emphasis was always placed, quite openly, in one or the other direction, with the pendulum—to no one's surprise—usually inclining to the German side.

Only for the best of the fifth generation (the sixth came too late) was the synthesis complete and its achievements of a lasting kind. To cite only the most significant, we think of the accomplishments of Leo Baeck and Martin Buber, in whose works the Jewish essence takes a German shape. Their works belong no less to the world than to the Jews. For Germans they are the heritage that has outlasted the catastrophe. It is for the Germans through their mediation to come to know Jewry as a whole, as a great historical realization of existence, and to recognize the nature of Jewish reality as it was lived in the world and in Germany, and thus to make up for the signal failure—the chief omission—of that period of 150–200 years when synthesis was the avowed aim. The synthesis was destroyed by the unbridled hatred of Jews just as its development was most promising. It would of necessity have let Judaism into German culture not as a gesture only but as real fact, not only as spiritual background but as theme and content.

Only then was there a symbiosis that had deep roots, a national faith, not a mere consent to or denial of assimilation. He who today approaches this memory, this aftermath, may himself chart the area of the synthesis. He will see that the works of Franz Kafka and Arnold Schönberg belong to it. Their art reveals its meaning only in the framework of the synthesis. They were personalities, these creators, but they expressed the spirit of their group. The humanely-inclined and the German sympathizers of the Jews have heretofore spoken only of individuals, of individual dedication in one or another of the politically acceptable modes of emancipation. The group was seen only by those who rejected or hated it, not by those who were sympathetic. No links of community were forged. If Germans lived with Jews, liked them, or, more rarely, loved them, they would have no kind of partnership except with Jews who had given up their essential Judaism or who were no longer Jews. It was the misfortune of the Jews that they did not or could not apprehend this. Rarely did Jews act naturally: they acted either out of a sense of oppression, or a too heady sense of liberation, and the mistakes that come in consequence were not forgiven them.

In Karlsbad in 1812, Goethe told the Prague Jew, Simon von Lämel:

> The predominant impression [of Jews] of my early youth in my home town was a terrible one. The figures from the dark, narrow Jewish quarter were strange, incomprehensible appearances which occupied my fantasy, but I could not understand how such a people could have produced from within it the most remarkable book in the world. What arose as disgust within me in my early youth was actually timidity before the mysterious and the ugly. My own scorn . . . was rather the reflection of the Christian men and women who surrounded me. It was only later, when I made the acquaintance of many sensitive and talented men of this tribe, that respect joined with my admiration for the people who created the Bible. [Teweles, p. 90.]

This contradictory feeling was characteristic of many Germans, especially of the most prominent, toward the Jews. This kind of relationship was hardly sound, and it remained unresolved. It could not be argued down by evidence of the happiest marriages between Christians and Jews or the happiest friendships. Instead of greater considerateness toward Jews for their mistakes the response was too frequently anger by Germans who neither despised nor oppressed them.

Most Jews sought Germany's affection. Germany's final reply to such attachment is outlined in the booklet, *Treason of the German Cause* by the Hölderlin scholar, Wilhelm Michel. In 1922 he knew what too few recognize today:

> That hatred for Jews is today the only point of reference common to all value judgments. It replaces religion for many—and we must bow our heads in shame in admitting this truth. [Michel, p. 9.]

BIBLIOGRAPHY

Sources Quoted in Text

Works of special importance for the understanding of the text are marked with an asterisk.

Anonymus, Die Unschuld der Jenseitigen, 1921
* *Baron S. W.*, Die Judenfrage auf dem Wiener Kongreß, 1920
Bloch J. S., Israel und die Völker, 1922
Brunner C., Höre Israel und höre Nicht-Israel, 1931
* *Buber M.*, Zion als Ziel und als Aufgabe, 1936
* *Cohen H.*, Deutschland und Judentum, 1916
Czermak E.—Karbach O., Ordnung in der Judenfrage, ca. 1933
Dinter A., Die Sünde wider das Blut, 12th ed., 1920
* *Dohm Ch. W.*, Über die bürgerliche Verbesserung der Juden, 3 volumes, 1781–1783
* *Dubnow S. M.*, Die neueste Geschichte des jüdischen Volkes [1789–1914], 3 volumes, 1920
* *Dühring E.*, Der Ersatz der Religion durch Vollkommeneres und die Ausscheidung alles Judenthums durch den modernen Völkergeist, 1883
* *Elbogen I.*, Geschichte der Juden in Deutschland, 1935
Feuchtwanger S., Die Judenfrage, 1916
Fontane Th., Der deutsche Krieg von 1866, 2 volumes
Fraenkel M., Jacob Bernays, 1932
* *Freund I.*, Die Emanzipation der Juden in Preußen, 2 volumes, 1912
* *Fritsch Th.*, Antisemiten-Katechismus, 19th ed., 1892
Geiger L., Die Deutsche Literatur und die Juden, 1910
Gorin bin M. J., Vom östlichen Judentum, 1918
* *Herzel Th.*, Der Judenstaat, 1897
* *Heß M.*, Rom und Jerusalem, new ed., 1935
Hirsch S. R., Chorev, Versuche über Jissroels Pflichten in der Zerstreuung, 1839
Hönigsberg v. S., Zur Judenfrage, 1848

* *Höxter J.*, Quellenbuch zur Jüdischen Geschichte und Literatur, Kleine Ausgabe, 1935
Jellinek A., Der jüdische Stamm, 1869
Kannengießer A., Juden und Katholiken in Österreich-Ungarn, 1896
* *Kobler F.*, Juden und Judentum in deutschen Briefen aus drei Jahrhunderten, 1935 [I]
* *Kobler F.*, Jüdische Geschichte in Briefen aus Ost und West, 1938 [II]
* *Kreppel J.*, Juden und Judentum, 1925
* Kriegsbriefe deutscher und österreichischer Juden, 1915 [I]
* Kriegsbriefe gefallener Deutscher Juden, 1935 [II]
Lagarde de P., Juden und Indogermanen, 1888
Liek D. W., Der Anteil des Judentums am Zusammenbruche Deutschlands, 1919
[*Löwenfeld R.*], Schutzjuden oder Staatsbürger?, 3rd ed., 1893
* *Marburg F.*, Der Antisemitismus in der Deutschen Republik, 1931
Max Prinz von Baden, Erinnerungen und Dokumente, 1928
* *Mendelssohns' M.*, Gesammelte Schriften, 7 Bände, 1843
* *Michel W.*, Verrat am Deutschtum, 1922
Mieses M., Der Ursprung des Judenhasses, 1923
Naudh H., Die Juden und der deutsche Staat, 1861
Palacký F., Geschichte von Böhmen
Pinsker L., Autoemanzipation, new ed., 1932
Popper-Lynkeus J., Fürst Bismarck und der Antisemitismus, 1925
Prinz J., Illustrierte jüdische Geschichte, 1930
* *Reichmann E. G.*, Flucht in den Haß, 1956
* *Rießer's G.*, Gesammelte Schriften, 4 volumes, 1867–1868
* *Scheuer O. F.*, Burschenschaft und Judenfrage, 1927
* *Schmidt H. D.*, The Terms of Emancipation, in Leo Baeck Institute Yearbook I, 1956
Siebert F., Der völkische Gedanke und die Verwirklichung des Zionismus, 1916
Stahl F. J., Der christliche Staat und sein Verhältnis zu Deismus und Judenthum, 1847
Steinthal H., Das auserwählte Volk oder Juden und Deutsche,

in "Allgemeine Zeitung des Judenthums," 1890, Nr. 17
* *Sterling E.*, Er ist wie du, 1956
Stöcker A., Das moderne Judenthum, 1880
Teweles H., Goethe und die Juden, 1925
* *Treitschke v. H.*, Ein Wort über unser Judenthum, 1880
Trietsch D., Juden und Deutsche, 1915
Valentin H., Antisemitenspiegel, 1937
Varnhagen R., Briefwechsel zwischen Rahel und David Veit, 1861
Varnhagen R., Rahel, Ein Buch des Andenkens für ihre Freunde, 3 volumes, 1834
Vollständige Verhandlungen des Ersten Vereinigten Preußischen Landtages über die Emancipationsfrage der Juden, 1847
Wagner R., Das Judenthum in der Musik, 1869
* *Wassermann J.*, Mein Weg als Deutscher und Jude, 1922
* *Weil B.*, K. C.-Jahrbuch, 1906
Wengeroff P., Memoiren einer Großmutter, 1922

Additional References

Adler-Rudel S., Ostjuden in Deutschland 1880–1940, 1959
Asaria Z., Die Juden in Köln, 1959
Auerbach L., Das Judenthum und seine Bekenner in Preußen und in den anderen Deutschen Bundesstaaten, 1890
Bender H., Der Kampf um die Judenemanzipation in Deutschland im Spiegel der Flugschriften 1815–1820, 1939
Böhm A., Die zionistische Bewegung, 2 volumes, 1935–1937
Coudenhove-Kalergi Graf H., Das Wesen des Antisemitismus, 1932 (Erstauflage 1901)
Eckstein A., Der Kampf der Juden um ihre Emanzipation in Bayern, 1905
Ehrlich E. L., Geschichte der Juden in Deutschland, 2nd ed., 1958
Goldschmidt H. L., Das Vermächtnis des deutschen Judentums, 1957
Graetz H., Geschichte der Juden von den ältesten Zeiten bis auf die Gegenwart, 2. Aufl., 1873–1900, II. Band: Geschichte

der Juden vom Beginn der Mendelssohnschen Zeit [1750] bis auf die neueste Zeit [1848]

Jöhlinger O., Bismarck und die Juden, 1921

Kohut A., Alexander von Humboldt und das Judentum, 1871

Lamm H. [Hrsg.], Von Juden in München, 1958

Leschnitzer A., Saul und David, Die Problematik der deutsch-jüdischen Lebensgemeinschaft, 1954

Lewin A., Geschichte der badischen Juden seit der Regierung Karl Friedrichs [1738–1809], 1909

Lichtheim R., Die Geschichte des deutschen Zionismus, 1954

Massing P. W., Rehearsal for Destruction, 1949

Michaelis A. [*Hrsg.*], Die Rechtsverhältnisse der Juden in Preußen seit dem Beginne des 19. Jahrhunderts, 1910

Naumann M., Von mosaischen und nicht-mosaischen Juden, 1921

Naumann M., Von Zionisten und Jüdischnationalen, 1921

Offenburg B., Das Erwachen des deutschen Nationalbewußtseins in der preußischen Judenheit, 1933

Ruppin A., Die Juden der Gegenwart, 1918

Ruppin A., Soziologie der Juden, 2 volumes, 1920

Schay R., Juden in der deutschen Politik, 1929

Seligmann C., Geschichte der jüdischen Reformbewegung von Mendelssohn bis zur Gegenwart, 1922

Sokolow N., Geschichte des Zionismus, 1920

Streckfuß K., Über das Verhältnis der Juden zu den christlichen Staaten, 1833

Tänzer A., Die Geschichte der Juden in Württemburg, 1937

Theilhaber F. A., Der Untergang der deutschen Juden, 2nd ed., 1921

Theilhaber F. A., Schicksal und Leistung, Juden in der deutschen Forschung und Technik, 1931

Tietze H., Die Juden Wiens, 1933

Wawrzinek K., Die Entstehung der deutschen Antisemitenparteien (1873–1890), 1927

Weil B., Der Weg der deutschen Juden, 1934

Wolbe E., Geschichte der Juden in Berlin und in der Mark Brandenburg, 1937

Zweig A., Bilanz der deutschen Judenheit, 1933

INDEX OF PLACE NAMES

INDEX OF PROPER NAMES